Preaching
for the Church
Today

Preaching for the Church Today

The Skills, Prayer, and
Art of Sermon Preparation

PAUL V. MARSHALL

THE CHURCH HYMNAL CORPORATION, NEW YORK

Scripture quotations are from the New Revised Standard Version
Bible, copyright 1989 by the Division of Christian Education
of the National Council of Churches of Christ in the
United States of America, and are used by permission.

The photograph on page 14 shows the reredos behind the High Altar of the
Washington National Cathedral. It was provided courtesy of the Cathedral,
and is used with their kind permission.

Dedication

To The Very Reverend James Corner Fenhagen,
and The Very Reverend Canon James Earl Annand.

Contents

Introduction

ermons are meeting places of theology and life. This work is meant to provide one way for that meeting to occur in a troubled church. The first part treats issues of learning itself and then of learning to preach, and goes on to present a capsule history and theology of preaching. Its intent is to help the reader set goals and also get some idea of how to reach them. The second part is the heart of the book, a practical treatment of getting sermons prepared, and some readers may in fact wish to start their reading with that section, which has its own little prolegomena on liturgy and preaching. The treatment of sermon preparation found there also lays emphasis on the cultivation and use of feedback. My present academic appointment is in "Worship and Pastoral Theology," and I try to show in what follows how these two disciplines intersect with homiletics in a way which can assist today's preacher. The method set out in Part Two has evolved in the classroom, and I have tried to illustrate key points with students' reports of their growth as preachers.

The book is addressed to all those who preach in Christian bodies which employ a lectionary and a liturgical year, and I have drawn upon examples from several denominations. In the few pages of discussion of "crisis" which take up a part of Chapter One, however, I have limited my observations to the Episcopal Church, not feeling free to comment on churches in whose ethos I do not live. At the same time, observation leads me to believe that the Episcopal Church's experience in recent years is similar to that of other Christian groups.

I have used the word "sermon" throughout. As far as I have been able to discover, "sermon" comes from the Latin and means word or discourse, while "homily" comes from the Greek and means discourse. Apparently at one point in the medieval west, a "homily" was a kind of "sermon" which addressed practical matters, especially moral concerns. The current popular distinction that a sermon is thoroughly prepared and longer, while the homily is informally prepared and shorter, has no relevance to the content of this book and is not observed in its pages. In reality it appears to be a distinction without a difference, and I have chosen not to trouble the reader with it in what follows.

In writing I have attempted to employ language which excludes no reader; however, I have not felt free to alter the words of others when borrowing their insights. Perhaps the occasionally resulting contrast can make clear how carefully preachers must search for words which do not get in the way of their message.

I must acknowledge some debts, particularly as the following chapters emphasize the importance of role models. George Hoyer gently taught hundreds of us to preach, and it is his "Main Idea and three P's" that I have developed in Chapter Six.

While he may not wish to recognize what has happened to the model here as his legitimate offspring, particularly with regard to the second and third "P's," I must gratefully acknowledge his influence in getting me to think in these terms. Gene Rooney guided me into the literature of neurolinguistics and helped me to see its usefulness for Christian ministry.

New Haven
St Andrew's Day, 1990

PART ONE

Of Preachers and Preaching

1. Liturgy, Crisis, and the Pulpit

The Liturgical Sermon Reconsidered

"I didn't take your course because I hate sermons about the reredos."[1]

With these words a student apologized for not having taken the course, "Preaching in the Liturgy," after hearing good things about it later on in the semester. There was for him, as there seems to be for many, the idea that there is "regular" preaching and then there is a special variety known as "liturgical" preaching. The latter is assumed to be either wooden exposition of the lectionary, or worse, preaching which is largely *about* the liturgy and its equipment, drawing most of its references from ecclesiastical furnishings

---

[1] As the reader may know, a reredos is the decorated panel behind an altar, often depicting Christ and the saints. Not a few examples are quite elaborate, often taking up much of the wall (see illustration, opposite).

such as a reredos, or still worse, liturgical minutiae from the history of worship. "Regular" preaching is assumed to be the meat and potatoes of proclamation, liturgical preaching its quiche.

The problem here is the assumed disjunction between preaching and liturgy, as though if either were given full expression, it could not coexist with the other. There is some historical justification for this view, mistaken as I believe it to be. There have been liturgical enthusiasts in several denominations who have little use for preaching, and there are entire church bodies for whom attending to the proclaimed word is the core of worship, and while sermons are to be carefully planned and often written out, they believe worship services usually ought not be. It is certainly not unknown for those with high personal investment in preaching or liturgy to mistrust the values and goals of those with opposite priorities.

It is possible to avoid this polarization, and possible to do so without giving short shrift to either preaching or worship. Consider the main topic of this book, the sermon in the Sunday assembly. Our century has seen ever-broadening Christian agreement on the centrality of the eucharist in the life of the church. Reforms of that liturgy have universally emphasized the belief that proclamation of the word is an integral part of eucharistic worship, and the first chapters of this book explore the implications of this fact in some detail. Here it is enough to note that preaching is increasingly seen as a liturgical act itself, a coordinated and functioning part of the liturgy. In the same way, liturgy is more and more understood to incorporate proclamation of the word as an essential activity. Rather than considering "liturgical preaching" as a variant on the norm for Christian proclamation, I am assuming here that preaching within and in relation to the worship of the church is the ordinary expression of Christian proclamation. There are and must be other expressions of proclamation as occasion and circumstance dictate, but for most preachers and most hearers, the sermon in the Sunday liturgy is their regular experience of proclamation.

The concern here, then, is not with the reredos or other hardware, but with the kind of preaching appropriate to the weekly gathering of Christians around word and sacrament. The concern is also with the special constraints that the liturgy puts upon preachers, and the special opportunities it offers them. The concern is about the kind of preaching that is fully integrated into the life and worship of the community. It is about preaching which is *of one piece* with the encounter with God and each other that Christians experience in liturgy. "Liturgical preaching," then, is preaching which is aware of the scriptural, ecclesiological, and sacramental context in which the Christian assembly gathers. It is congruent with that setting and works to unite its parts in the hearer's experience for the building up of the faithful and the service of the world. To that end, when appropriate, it may even mention the reredos.

Crisis as Opportunity

Most people acknowledge that mainline American religion is in a period of crisis. A case in point is my own denomination, and I consider it in the next few paragraphs as the example I know best. I do so in the belief that readers of other mainstream Christian bodies will recognize their own churches' patterns of behavior in what I describe. Since the publication of John Booty's *The Episcopal Church in Crisis,* there has developed in that church a small industry devoted to diagnosing the causes of the current crisis and prescribing for it. "Cures" recently recommended in church journals include less preaching and more adult education, both more prayer book reform and the undoing of prayer book reform, and the evangelization of the Jews. Occasionally there have also appeared the views of those who insist that there is no crisis, and that things are in fact just fine. Every set of numbers receives several interpretations, and accounts of declining parishes are countered with reports of those experiencing renewed vigor. Opinion polls have even been employed to investigate the attitudes of those members still active. Most of the responses seem largely concerned for the future of the church as institution.

Institutional survival is not what the "crisis" is really about, however. In its original sense, the word crisis means a point of judgment, a point of evaluating performance and deciding identity and future direction. Times when the institution appears to be in danger of disappearing are times of crisis in the best sense: they force all but the most unthinking or insecure to ask what the institution is for, and whether it is effective in meeting its purpose. The drop in both numbers and apparent influence in the world offers Christians an opportunity to regroup around the basic functions of the church and to reappropriate energy to them in ways that serve its mission.

One of the responses to the crisis as the Episcopal Church has experienced it troubles me more than all the rest. I have encountered it several times in the pronouncements of church leaders, and saw it quoted in the *New York Times* (16 October 1989) in an article which also explained, entirely in passing, that the Episcopal Church was once an important force in New York life. It is the idea that all will be well if the Episcopal Church simply "keeps on doing what it does well," by which is meant emphasizing its talents for liturgy and the fostering of personal spirituality in the Benedictine tradition.

There are two ways to question this approach, ways which do not detract from the importance of liturgy and spiritual formation. The first is purely theological. I am sure that those who propose this "keep on" response would agree that the Christian Church is to have a mission, a job to do in the world. In that case they might agree that the prescription simply to "keep on" assumes that the church's mission does not have to be given priority in evaluating our performance, or that the nature of the world might mean adjusting our emphasis if we are to be faithful to our calling. This position seems to assume that the Episcopal Church is to limit its outreach to those who are already Christian and now seek depth in their experience of public and private prayer in what has already been termed an ecclesiastical finishing school by its critics. Worse, the position encourages the wearing of partisan and historical blinders. It ignores utterly the existence of the strong preaching tradition of the Evangelical wing in the Episcopal Church, and does not acknowledge what that tradition has to contribute to its understanding of how it is to carry out its central mission.

In the most general terms, the mission of Christianity can be described as offering to all people that fullness of life in God available to disciples of Jesus Christ, and witnessing to Jesus' call for everyone to enact God's compassion and justice in the world. Such a mission cannot be performed without intense self-awareness. Hence I am much more troubled by the practical implications of the suggestion that we simply keep on keeping on. It epitomizes what I have come to call the great American failure trap: *if something does not work, do it more.* Take youth as an example at home and church. Parents whose children do not respond to discipline often think that the solution lies in more discipline. The frustration—and occasional tragedy—that such an approach yields are too well known to require comment here. In the same vein, congregations whose conventional youth programs are dropping off tend think that the answer is *more* conventional youth programs, and seldom examine current values and social realities which may require different approaches. At its worst, the "do it more" syndrome assumes that the answers and the questions never change, and the baby is kept in aging and soiled bath water that may kill it, or in a tub it outgrew years ago and which now stunts its further growth.

In opposition to the "do it more" fallacy, there lies the truth of the *law of requisite variety:* those who have the most options succeed. The chess player who has the most moves in her repertoire wins. Those who face a crisis as a time to assess, learn, and attempt to change for the better, are the ones likely to make the helpful contribution.

To use the law of requisite variety means being honest: learn from mistakes and wrong turns, and learn to part with what has become obsolete. All feedback is valuable. In addition to finding the right filament for the first electric light, Thomas Edison was quite proud of the fact that he also had learned the properties of some two thousand filaments that did not work for that particular application, and thought it was important to say so.

Thus the gift of mainline Christianity's present crisis is that we are in a position to affirm the many liturgical and spiritual treasures of our heritage, and also to announce that just possessing them is not enough to guarantee our survival—or our right to survive—in the present world. We must choose the right strategies for our time.

In addition, if we are to perform the mission the New Testament gives, we have got to be better at making explicit connections between people's lives as they are, and the kind of life God offers in Christ. In general, that means teaching, spiritual formation, and guided experience in discipleship: here it means that we can focus more of our attention on preaching that matters to people. From the point of view of homiletics, our recent pattern of pretty much anything-goes in preaching does not appear to have gotten the results we want. It probably needs to be filed away with our set of other non-illuminating filaments for possible use at another time. In its place we can develop preaching which both enriches the faithful and invites the outsider to Christian life.

I must make an important distinction here. The troubles of the church have been for some an opportunity to grind axes and find other people to blame. The church press has at times looked like a repeated scene from Laurel and Hardy, only with both characters saying to each other, "This is a fine mess *you've* gotten us in."

I do not believe that such an attitude is productive, or even accurate. Like Edison searching for the right filament without feeling like a failure over the ones that had other value than illumination, we now begin to know that something needs to be added or reaffirmed, not that something needs to be rejected or punished.

The particular victim of the search for scapegoats seems to be the emphasis the church has put on the social implications of Christian faith. My own view is that most of what the church has explored and undertaken in the last thirty years has been very valuable, even when in hindsight perhaps mistaken upon occasion, and in intention always very faithful to our identity as disciples of Jesus serving the world in his name. Christian bodies have taken chances, a rare and valuable trait in religious institutions, as they try to address our age. The value of the fact that American Christians have been forced by history to create an atmosphere where passionate disagreement is possible cannot be underestimated.

This book is not written because I think that Christians need to regret the experiments of the last decades. It is written because I think that from a tactical point of view we could be a lot better at connecting the broad range of church positions and programs to the basic Christian beliefs on which they are founded. Tactically, we can be better at showing people that the foundations are there, functioning and nourishing behind and within church program. For example, as a student of liturgy I take comfort in the way modern baptismal rites make just such a connection liturgically. In one piece we celebrate personal conversion, God's regenerative grace, our commitment to sacramental and doctrinal growth, and also affirm explicitly and as mandatory the living out of relationship to Christ in the ministries of witness, service and justice. Our doctrine in these rites is that faith in Jesus, personal spirituality, and service to the world are parts of one reality, parts which need and support each other. Our doctrine is that Christian living is the most important and exciting thing one can undertake in this world, the most holistic approach to human existence that there is. I believe that in our preaching we must also show that connectedness between spiritual reality and public life, and must show people how it can work in their lives. Making such connections in sermons and teaching may not in fact be the one thing we are always good at, but it is the one thing Christians are called to do above all else. All the rest flows from it.

In sum, experience suggests that we will do better at helping the faithful to be faithful if we make more explicit and inviting the *connection* of the church's activities to its identity in Jesus Christ. Not the only answer, but one answer or part of an answer to the Crisis is to be more forthcoming about the Gospel, and to do it in words and in ways that contemporary Christians can hear. This means that preaching style may have to change.

Many preachers think, in fact they know, that they have been trying to say the Gospel, trying to make connections, trying to share their vision, and yet have come away somewhat frustrated. Why?

Variety of personality type seems to be part of the answer. Many readers are already familiar with the Jungian categories on which the Meyers-Briggs indicator is based, so we follow its major metaphors here. According to this most widely used system of studying personality differences, some people get their ideas all at once, others need to have evidence laid out bit by bit. Some people prefer firm and lasting decisions while others like to keep their options open as long as possible. Some people value logic in making decisions, others put a great deal of emphasis on personal values. According to a very large bank of data, most clergy are intuitives, "big picture" people who get ideas pretty much all at once.[2] Within the ranks of the clergy, these intuitive types are also often "perceivers" who often prefer a personal and, in our case, a homiletical style which is very open-ended, non-directive, and almost always receptive to the new and inspiring. Indisputably, such intuitive preachers are by inclination and training in a position to make an enormous contribution to the church as prophets and teachers, helping us to explore the new age which the ministry of Jesus opened up for us.

These preachers often experience frustration because the

---

[2] The mass of data is best applied to our subject in Roy Oswald and Otto Kroeger, *Personality Type and Religious Leadership* (Washington: The Alban Institute, 1988).

1. Liturgy, Crisis, and the Pulpit   **23** sizeable majority of parishioners take in and decide about information in another way. The "sensates," these listeners prefer to apprehend reality not in big picture flashes, but by taking in data through the senses, in discrete pieces. In addition, many of them have a preference for the logical and practical, for the things they can rely on to work, and for ends they believe to be valuable.

Whose system of handling information is to prevail in the sermon? It seems easier for the intuitive preacher to learn to speak the language of the predominantly sensate flock than to expect three hundred or so parishioners to learn to decode an intuitive sermon.[3]

Assuming for the sake of argument that intuitives are "right," and what sensate listeners need is to have their imaginations stimulated and their passions stirred, contact has to be made with them in their "language," with structure and order. Sensate listeners need to know why it is (and it *is*) a good idea to dream dreams and see visions, and then be helped to go about doing it. Thus this book can be for preachers an exercise in the law of requisite variety: it suggests that when intuitive preaching is not working, they do not have to find ways to become more intuitive in preaching, but may rather try something different, what we will call connectedness.

The need to convey the excitement and possibilities of Christian life along with its unshakeable foundations and sure hope is the reason that what follows is about stimulating the preacher's intuition and insight. It is also about logical and connected sermon construction. When the connections are made, and the value of the vision conveyed clearly, the largely

---

[3] There are situations where the opposite applies. In moving from a parish to a theological school, I am working hard at becoming fluent in the language of an overwhelmingly intuitive-feeling student body.

sensate faithful enter the effort with enormous commitment, energy, and perseverance.

This book is not just about how to preach to sensates, and attention is paid later to the trap of piling up bits of data in sermons (i.e., boring people to death). I am proposing a method which helps intuitives communicate their visions in terms accessible to sensates. I am also proposing ways in which more sensate preachers can gain access to their intuitive faculties and help others to do the same. Ideally, the book works to help sensates see visions and intuitives to get organized.

Preachers Are Made, Not Born

There is nothing more offensive than hearing a preacher elevate personal preferences to the status of virtue. Much of what follows flows from a sensate, how-to-do-it perspective, and thus some people will find the method easier to follow than others. I offer it as strategy, not as a doctrine. Oswald and Kroeger, both intuitive feeling types, believe intuitives are more likely to be strong preachers.[4] Nonetheless, they confess, when discussing another aspect of personalty, the closure/openness dimension ("J/P" in Meyers-Briggs terms) alluded to above, that "Our homiletics professors were wise to hammer at us the importance of having an outline, planning a beginning and an ending, writing out a manuscript, getting it organized." I am adding that the hammering has to be about more than organization. What the typical parishioner needs is the connection, the relevance, in fact the *use* of what is being said, while it seems that very many preachers experience a sense of completion just in sharing the

---

[4] Oswald and Kroeger, p. 55.

vision, the excitement. They are puzzled, sometimes hurt and judgmental, when hearers do not automatically share their enthusiasm. When the connections are not made, the majority of hearers tend to feel that their time is wasted and may tune out, perhaps missing a great moment of vision. Worse, sensates can be overwhelmed by too big a picture and despairingly decide "it is high, I cannot attain unto it."

This book is intended particularly for new preachers, but also for those who want to rethink their own method of sermon preparation. Its primary audience is those for whom preaching will be part of a pastoral and liturgical ministry on a full-time basis, for the most part clergy and clergy-to-be. Increasingly churches provide for the organized training and licensing of lay preachers, and this book is offered with them in mind as well. It describes a set of skills, and offers a specimen method which some seminarians have found helpful over a dozen years. I offer it because I find that it has worked.

The emphasis on method and technique may need some comment. The comment is necessary because preaching sermons is, in the end, a very individual thing. So are playing golf, writing music, and selling real estate. But none of them is a very individual thing in the beginning. In each case personal creativity takes over within a complex of technical skills gained over hundreds or thousands of hours. Technique then no longer has primary place in consciousness, if it is conscious at all, because it has been thoroughly learned. The basis for creativity is skill.

This chapter was begun two days after the death of the great pianist Vladimir Horowitz. His death brings to mind the time that someone supposedly said to the younger Horowitz: "Oh, Mr. Horowitz, I'd give anything to play the piano the way you do."

Horowitz shot back: "No, you wouldn't."

Pressed for an explanation, Horowitz is remembered as

saying: "If you would give anything, you would already have given it. To play as I do takes only eight hours of practice every day of your life for forty-five years."

Leaving aside the question of enormous intellects, rare prodigies, and several tragic forms of autism, much of the research done on genius and creativity indicates that Horowitz was right. "All" that people must do in order to do something extremely well is have an intense desire to do it, a positive role model, very positive images of themselves succeeding—and the discipline to invest many hours learning and polishing.

This emphasis on technique is meant as encouragement for those for whom preaching seems to be an overwhelming or impossible task. It can be learned, one step at a time. The emphasis on discipline is meant as encouragement for those for whom getting things done is not always easy: discipline itself can be learned and filled with meaning when it is understood as a means to attaining an important goal.

When one merges what behavioral psychology has discovered about the pattern of success with what we know about the traditions of spirituality, a powerful tool for effective discipline emerges. If the goal of preaching is to equip the saints for ministry, and if to bring others to faith is a part of one's deepest prayers, the intense desire scientists speak of is not only generated, but becomes a permanent part of how one listens and thinks throughout the day. That desire then produces sermons which are congruent with the soul of the preacher. Here our concern is precisely the opposite of "coming up with" a sermon. The idea is to be constantly "going down to" the depths of one's experience to become a conscious part of God's desire to realize the created intent of human existence. That provides the existential quality of commitment which successful athletes and business people usually call "fire in the belly," an expression that readily connects with religious symbols.

The next step in the pattern of effectiveness is selection of role models. In your experience, who has shown the kind of commitment to and excellence in preaching that occasioned change in your life? Whose writings have stirred you to faith and discipleship, or to the desire to preach effective sermons? Each of us will have a different list, but it is important that we each have such a roster. Mine includes professors and clergy whose preaching has brought change in my life. It also includes figures of the past and present whom I only know by their writings, preachers such as Donne, Herbert, Gossip, Tillich and King. I try to preach in their company, without worrying about preaching at their level. The frequent references to George Herbert's *The Country Parson* in this book indicate the degree to which he has become my companion as I preach and think about preaching.[5]

The usefulness of the role model is hardly a twentieth century discovery. For example, when seeking to turn ordinary believers into dedicated and persevering disciples, the writer to the Hebrews asks them to have a composite image of faithfulness. It is an image remarkably like that which our behavioral scientists are now discovering to be so powerful. In Hebrews the trusting and persevering saints of the past are brought into focus by name and capsule biography as examples of and encouragement to faith and commitment in the present. They are then re-imaged as the crowd in a stadium (the meaning of "cloud of witnesses"), cheering Christians on as they strip for the "game." Above all, the writer offers Jesus, not only as role model *par excellence*, but as "pioneer" and guarantor that beyond the struggle there is set great joy. How do you populate the stadium

---

[5] A good modern edition is John Wall, ed., *George Herbert. The Country Parson, The Temple* (New York: Paulist Press, 1981.)

crowd as you prepare to preach? Who can you imagine as cheering you on?

Perhaps the part of the current psychological formula for success most likely to encounter resistance is the prescription that preachers have a strong mental image of themselves succeeding. Remnants of unhelpful piety tend to quash ambition and visions of success, and they need to be addressed. Consider how one preacher faced just this.

Martin Luther King, Jr., addressed the issue of ambition and drive for success in the famous sermon, "The Drum Major Instinct." King mixed the stories of Philip and James asking about seating in the Messianic throne room with the image of the drum major leading a parade. King rejected the conventional sublimation of the instinct to be out front, an affectation of the servile piety of a modern Uriah Heep. Instead, he transformed the urge, and made it all right for Christians to reach for the top energetically, identifying greatness with joining the One who came not to be served, but to serve. His utterly sensate conclusion admits to and celebrates his "ambition":

> If any of you are around when I have to meet my day, I don't want a long funeral. And if you get somebody to deliver the eulogy, tell them not to talk too long. . . . Tell them not to mention that I have a Nobel Peace Prize, that isn't important. Tell them not to mention that I have three or four hundred other awards, that's not important. Tell them not to mention where I went to school.
>
> I'd like somebody to mention that day, that Martin Luther King, Jr. tried to give his life serving others. I'd like for somebody to say that day, that Martin Luther King, Jr. tried to love somebody. I want you to say that day, that I tried to be right on the war question. I want you to be able to say on that day, that I did try, in my life, to clothe those who were naked. I want you to say, on that day, that I did

try, in my life, to visit those who were in prison. I want you to say that I tried to love and serve humanity.

Yes, if you want to say that I was a drum major, say that I was a drum major for righteousness. And all of the other shallow things will not matter. I won't have any money to leave behind. I won't have the fine and luxurious things of life to leave behind. But I just want to leave a committed life behind. . . .

Yes, Jesus, I want to be on your right side or your left side, not for any selfish reason. I want to be on your right or your best side, not in terms of some political kingdom or ambition, but I just want to be there in love and in justice and in truth and in commitment to others, so that we can make this old world a new one.[6]

Put this way, why not dare to imagine a career as a "great" preacher?

This book, then, is about work, about the discipline that arises not from duty or careerism. That discipline arises from the experience of being loved by God and in turn loving God and God's people. Desire, role model, and image of success make the discipline possible. But that discipline ultimately arises from the conviction that God calls people—you and me—and empowers them to speak to and for the church.

---

6 "The Drum Major Instinct" may be found in *Testament of Hope: The Essential Writings of Martin Luther King, Jr.* (San Francisco: Harper and Row, 1986).

2. | Parish Preaching

here are many ways to approach the task of preaching, and many models which work quite effectively. The one explored here takes its agenda from the great English liturgical reform of the 1930s, the "Parish Communion" movement. It is to that movement that Christians of many stripes owe much that we take for granted in our worship today. Before turning to it, some general orientation to liturgical proclamation is in order.

Origins of the Liturgical Address

The liturgical address is not commonly encountered in the world's religions. It belongs chiefly to "religions of the book," and then principally to Judaism and Christianity. The address in Christian liturgy comes from a Jewish ancestor, the sermon in the Sabbath morning synagogue service. We do not know precisely how the synagogue liturgy was celebrated in the ancient world, but it appears that the first scripture reading was a passage of the Torah. A portion of the Psalter was next, followed by a selection from one of the prophets. These portions were followed by an address or commentary. The method of selecting preachers, if there was general organization, is not known, but it seems clear the preaching was not the task of the *archisynagogus* who presided over the liturgy, at least not necessarily. Nor was preaching limited to local religious officials: Jesus preached in the Nazareth synagogue, and Paul made it his practice to speak in the synagogues wherever he went.

Jewish Christians maintained their formal connections with the synagogue as long as that was possible; therefore it is not surprising that we can detect the synagogue pattern of readings followed by comment in those distinctly Christian meetings described in the Acts of the Apostles. By the time of Justin Martyr this pattern had become the first half of a two-part Lord's Day liturgy of word and sacramental meal. This is Justin's description of the liturgy of the word in the middle of the first century:

> On the day called the day of the Sun, an assembly is held in one place of all who live in town and country, and the memoirs of the apostles and the writings of the prophets are read as long as time allows. Then, when the lector has finished, the president in a discourse admonishes us to imitate these good things. *(I Apol. 67)*

The inherited synagogue pattern is clear, but in Justin's report there is a distinct shift: the president of the assembly is also the preacher. What other titles the president might have had at that point in the development of Justin's Christian community at Rome is not known, but from him we learn that besides preaching, the president gave thanks over the bread and cup. Whether "bishop," "presbyter," or one of the last of itinerant "prophets," this early celebrant expressed presidency directly in the capstone of each part of the liturgy, by both preaching and offering the eucharistic prayer.

As church offices became regularized, and the prophetic vocation more institutionalized, the bishop emerged as the one who performed the double ministry of preaching and offering the great thanksgiving. The association of the task of preaching at the liturgy with the episcopate, to the exclusion of other orders, was so strong that sometimes scandal arose when permission to preach at the liturgy was granted to presbyters, as it was in the cases of Origen and Augustine. The liturgy of the late fourth century *Apostolic Constitutions* (II, 57, 5-9) indicates that at that time in the East, presbyters might speak at the liturgy if they had anything to say, but when they were through speaking the bishop preached the sermon. In the West, however, presbyters were not given such an opportunity, and the speaker at the eucharist was the bishop. One of the reasons given for this development was the current belief that unlike bishops, presbyters could not be counted upon to avoid heresy.

A tightly-knit eucharistic assembly of "all who live in town and country," centered in the ministry of the bishop, was not possible as Christianity grew, and it was not even thinkable in the huge missionary territories that eventually opened in the post-Constantinian era, particularly in the country north of the Alps. Thus, at the Council of Vaison (529), for instance, presbyters were given permission to preach at the eucharists over which they presided. The result was that in the absence of the bishop, a unified ministry of word and sacrament was maintained by accompanying the presbyteral mass with the presbyteral sermon.

This connection that the early church perceived between preaching and presidency at the eucharist is reflected in the present Roman and Lutheran eucharistic rites which stipulate that ordinarily the celebrant is to be the preacher. It is debatable whether or not this ought to be the norm today, to be sure, but it is clear that Christians, ancient and modern, have detected an intimate theological link between word and sacrament, one to which we shall return.

The amount of preaching which was done in the Sunday assembly fell off almost in proportion to the growth of Christianity. This is not to say that preaching was not done, but that it disappeared from the eucharist to a large extent as Sunday masses multiplied and the level of clerical learning became very uneven. As the spoken liturgy performed by a single person became the rule rather than the exception, preaching at the eucharist virtually disappeared.

There were revivals of preaching during the Middle Ages, including lay preaching movements, but lay and monastic preachers primarily held forth outside of the liturgy, often outside the walls of the parish church. These "mission" sermons were primarily devotional or moral rather than expository or doxological. Deprived of a liturgical setting, these sermons soon developed little liturgies of their own, surrounding proclamation with prayers and other devotions.

At the time of the Reformation, with its great reemphasis on preaching, Luther attempted to restore the sermon to its original liturgical context. Although the reformers tried to bring preaching to their worship services, and even made it the chief feature of many of them, it was the friars' extra-liturgical sermon and accompanying devotions that they took as model for context and content of the "preaching service." Thus it was that the sermon detached from the eucharistic liturgy became the common type of preaching in the Protestant churches, complete with para-liturgical acts to precede and follow it. Rationalism, Pietism, and the rigors of the American frontier widened the perceptual gap between preaching and liturgy. Even in the "liturgical" branches of non-Roman Christianity, the sermon developed as a stand-alone item. The result was that for Episcopalians, for example, the idea of advertising a service as "Holy Communion with Sermon" became thinkable.

An Emerging Consensus

The last hundred years have witnessed a development beyond that point, however. The call for a renewal of preaching in this period is more than simply a call to have holy communion with sermons. It is a call to view preaching as a liturgical act, related to the whole of liturgical celebration, liturgical texts and the church year, all for the assistance and direction of the assembly in its work of praise and discipleship.

The concept of a "liturgical sermon" is in some respects new and in others related to patristic and Reformation emphasis. It is certainly ecumenical. The principles affirmed in the *Constitution on the Sacred Liturgy* of Vatican II and confirmed in Paul VI's "General Instruction" in the Roman Missal are also found in the liturgical books of other western Christian communities.

The Roman Catholic view may surprise many a "Protestant":

Christ himself is present in his word, since it is he himself who speaks when the holy scriptures are read in the church. . . . In the liturgy God speaks to his people and Christ is still proclaiming his Gospel. . . . The sermon is part of the liturgical service . . . the ministry of preaching is to be fulfilled with exactness and fidelity. The sermon, moreover, should draw its content mainly from scriptural and liturgical sources, and its character should be that of proclamation of God's wonderful works in the history of salvation, the mystery of Christ, ever made present and active with us, especially in the celebration. . . . By means of the homily the mysteries of the faith and guiding principles of the Christian life are expounded from the sacred text, during the course of the liturgical year; the homily therefore, is to be highly esteemed as part of the liturgy itself; in fact, at Masses which are celebrated . . . on Sundays it should not be omitted except for serious reason. . . . It is to be given on Sundays and holy days . . . at all Masses which are celebrated with a congregation. It is recommended on other days, especially on the weekdays of Advent, Lent, and Easter, as well as on other feasts and occasions when the people come to church in large numbers. (*Constitution on the Sacred Liturgy* 4,33,35. ii, 52; "General Instruction," 42.)

The *Lutheran Book of Worship* takes a similar view:

The Holy Communion has two principal parts: One centers in proclamation of the Word through the reading of the Scriptures and preaching: the other centers in sharing the sacramental meal. Surrounded by prayer, praise, and thanksgiving, these two parts are so intimately connected as to form one unified act of worship. . . . The presiding minister is usually the preacher. . . . Only under extraordinary circumstances would the sermon be omitted from this service. (*Minister's Desk Edition,* 25, 27.)

The 1979 *Book of Common Prayer* acknowledges rubrically no situation in which the sermon is omitted from the eucharist, reflecting the thought of Anglicans such as Norman Pittenger:

The Lord's Supper is integrally bound up with the proclamation of the gospel, so that either one of them without the other is truncated and partial. It is not that the gospel adds anything to the sacrament, or the sacrament adds anything to the gospel; it is simply that they belong together, that together they make *one thing*—and that one thing is the Lord Jesus Christ, in whom God so richly and truly dwelt for the wholeness of man. This is why the normal worship of the Christian should be the combined ministry of Word and Sacrament. Sunday by Sunday, as Christ's people come to worship God, they should hear the word and receive the sacrament; and by these two, which are really one, be built up in Christ their Lord and their Life, by whom through Word and Sacrament they are nourished and strengthened for Christian witness as "faithful soldiers and servants of Christ, until their life's end."[7]

This view is common even among less liturgically-oriented denominations. The Reformed scholar Jean-Jacques von Allmen takes much the same position, and we may recall Calvin's unsuccessful attempts to convince the Geneva authorities that the separation of word and sacrament is "a vicious practice." Karl Barth went so far as to suggest that churches be furnished in such a way that word and sacrament be encountered in the same place, and proposed a table with a (removable) reading desk atop it to serve as both pulpit and altar.

Parish Communion, Parish Sermon

A. G. Hebert and others associated with him valued nineteenth century attempts to reclaim the riches of Christian worship.[8]

---

[7] W. Norman Pittenger, *Proclaiming Christ Today*, (Greenwich: Seabury, 1962) p. 94.

[8] I must here give woefully short shrift to a major force in the Anglicanism of the 1930s-1950s. The interested reader is encouraged to consult the original collection of essays, edited by Hebert and entitled *The Parish Communion*

They were particularly concerned to make those riches accessible to ordinary worshippers so that the eucharist could once again become the foundation of the English church's spiritual life. In those days most Anglo-Catholic parishes had their principal celebration in the late morning, and added to the service's length with elaborate, even operatic, musical settings. Such length discouraged family attendance. The late hour discouraged frequent communion, as fasting from midnight was also required of communicants, and few English people of that time were willing to do without their traditional Sunday breakfast until 1 P.M. A baroque ceremonial style, and a liturgy conducted at great physical distance from the nave, gave the impression that the liturgy was principally *for* and entirely *about* the clergy, anyway. For reasons that Hebert and others considered utterly inessential, people were staying away from eucharistic worship in large numbers.

Several things marked the Parish Communion movement in its attempt to remedy the situation. Musical settings of the service were more straightforward, and congregational participation singing the liturgy was encouraged in many places. The 11 A.M. service times were moved back to 9:00 or 9:30. What we know as the offertory procession was eventually introduced in some places, with lay people bearing the gifts. Ceremonial was not less reverent or significant, but it often became less complex. In some places nave altars were installed in their pre-Reformation places at the crossing. These and other factors all led to a different perception of the eucharist. No longer the clergy's domain, the service was increasingly perceived by the assembly as "our" celebration, although certainly the clergy continued to

---

(London: SPCK, 1937), as well as Donald Gray, *Earth and Altar*, (Norwich, U.K.: The Canterbury Press, 1986).

perform all the roles which are appropriate to ordained ministry. The movement rendered the sacrament more accessible to Christ's people, and many more found it possible to join in the offering of the eucharist and to receive communion on a regular basis. In a time when changing a word of the liturgy was illegal in England, its *circumstances* were adjusted so as to give it greater effectiveness in shaping the life of the church at large.

I have tried to develop a similar model for the "parish sermon," operating along lines parallel to those Hebert and his associates followed in liturgical work. In this model it is assumed that preaching is indeed primarily, but not exclusively, a clerical task. Nonetheless, its application does not produce a clerical or clericalizing sermon. Elaborate ceremonial, much of it unseen by congregation, was arguably for the ministers of the mass of the ritualistic period of Anglicanism. In the same way, sermons devoted to the preacher's special gifts and personality, sermons which focus attention on the cleverness or wisdom or holiness of the preacher instead of the lives of the hearers in encounter with God, may be considered preacher-centered, which usually means clericalized. There is a self-referential quality in much of today's preaching which suggests that the sermon is an act of therapy rather than proclamation, the great cloud of witnesses being lost in the miasmal mists of the analyst's couch or the smoke-filled rooms of self-help groups.

That being said, it should be immediately noted that I propose a method which is intensely personal in the initial stages, a method which utilizes the person of the preacher fully, but one which also encourages daily wrestling with the scriptural truth that it is not ourselves that we preach. In *The Country Parson,* George Herbert describes the preacher as doing intense personal work, even using as his first tool in interpreting the scriptures a "holy life." Ultimately in his sermon what he shared were the "comforts" he had found in such a way that other people could appropriate them. Quite clearly, we live in a time when telling one's "story" is a great homiletical concern, and we shall return to that later. What is asked of storytellers here is that they tell their story in such a way as to invite others into the story in order to focus on the power, comfort, direction, strength, and discipleship they have discovered.

In terms of our parallel with the Parish Communion, we are seeking a sermon which engages the hearers and directs their attention to their own lives and commitments, not the preacher's. To do this, some techniques are used, and some rhetorical fireworks sacrificed for the goal of building up the body of Christ. The sermon is ultimately not "for" the preacher any more than the eucharist is for the celebrant. Both are for the glory of God and the good of the assembly; both are much more than, but may not ever be less than, pastoral tools. Stewardship of either is a great privilege, and also a great trust.

This pastoral nature of the "parish sermon" is one of the reasons we shall pay so much attention to the self of the preacher in what follows. This concern grew from a visit I had with German homiletics professors in 1980. They were at that time coming to terms with a study of some thousands of European parishioners, Protestant and Catholic, which revealed a startling piece of information. The single thing the hearers most remembered about sermons was not the content, but how the preacher seemed to feel that day in relation to self, the world, and the hearers. Further, preachers were not rated good or bad in terms of their erudition, wit, wisdom, or knowledge of the Bible. What mattered to people was the extent to which they indicated that they valued and trusted their hearers. In other words, for these hearers, before biblical insight and pastoral wisdom can be received, the preacher must establish basic rapport. The reader is invited to begin thinking about this in preparation for the later discussion of why in the Christian apprehension of salvation history it was not prophecy but incarnation which made change possible for people.

There are four key elements in the parish sermon constructed on this model.

1. *The parish sermon is a pastoral application of a relevant Christian truth to the worship and lives of the hearers.* Worship and life are one piece here. For those who are re-created in Christ, all of life is an act of worship, a living sacrifice, a truth which is given pointed expression and particular direction and impetus in the Sunday eucharist.

The idea that the application be pastoral is to insist that the sermon be preached out of genuine concern for the well-being of the hearers and for their growth into the fullness of maturity in Christ. This demands some identification with their lot in life, and rules out an Olympian stance for the preacher.

I am placing relevance next to truth here precisely to check sermons in which references to the reredos (or to the political situation) are made without their having any useful point. Many of us do indeed enjoy knowing things for the joy of knowing them, but particularly in an age when most people devote little time beyond an hour in church to their development as Christians, the Sunday sermon cannot be the usual place to provide that joy. In a battle against principalities and powers, the truths that are spoken need to equip, direct, and sustain those who live on the front lines. The reredos and other liturgical equipment sometimes do just that, but for this model of preaching, the preacher needs to make the connection explicitly.

Christianity is placed between relevance and truth because even less than sermons about the reredos do we need sermons about the sunset in Jerusalem or home life in Bible times. The sunset or ancient domestic arrangements may help illustrate a useful sermon, but the focus needs to be on our growth into the full stature of Christ and what that concept means in the world today. This is most definitely not to say that preaching is a weekly exercise in converting the faithful, but it is to insist that whatever the sermon examines needs to be brought under the lens of our identity as Christians. Whether the sermon is about AIDS or Rogation Days, nuclear power or speaking in tongues, the connection to Christian faith must be made, or we risk losing our audience, our voice, and our justification for taking up people's time. The connection may be as simple as pointing out that as Christians who believe themselves to be stewards of our planet's environment, we must examine certain issues. The connection may also be as profound as showing how an incarnational religion cannot join in the hate and judgmentalism surrounding tragic illness, but must be involved in the actual care of those who suffer, and thus leading its adherents to discover identity with Christ in a deeper way.

2. *The parish sermon has one clearly defined objective.* This objective is called the Main Idea in subsequent chapters.

Sermons of an hour or so in length have not been popular for some time now. In the 15 to 20 minutes that most congregations are conditioned to expect, exploring one point well is the best course. The preacher is helped by having that objective in mind *and on paper* before writing: it provides an organizational principle and also filters out extraneous and distracting ideas.

It also encourages honesty and clarity within the preacher. If your real goal in a sermon is to get people *to understand* your witness, or *to give* more money, or *to believe* in the value of the apostolic ministry, or *to work* for better care of the elderly, write that down at the head of your working papers, and develop a strategy for presenting the value of and means to that behavior to the hearers.

3. *The sermon does not violate the Christian message in its method.* To speak of behavioral objectives is to invite temptation to coercion and manipulation. Christians are known to have

fallen into the traps of manipulating each other by anger, guilt, and appeals to idolatrous values such as the "honor of God" (the Crusades) or institutional survival (the last thirty years). If we imagine ourselves, as St. Paul did, as those through whom God is making an appeal, our words and tactics need to be consistent with what we know about God in Christ, and how in fact God makes change possible in our lives.

This does not mean that sin is not confronted or that costly love is not urged. It is not an invitation to preach overly tentative sermons couched in the subjunctive mood. It does envision adult Christians presenting to other adult Christians what they believe to be important truths in a way that respects the integrity and value of the hearers while maintaining the urgency of the message. The sermon does not infantilize the hearers or make them dependent upon clerical approval or "strokes," but shows them ways to develop as useful agents of God's rule in this world.

4. *The sermon is part of a pastoral relationship.* Preachers sometimes say things in sermons that they would never say to one or two people, face to face. The elevated position and protective walls of the pulpit, along with the pretended anonymity of the audience invite a lot of hash-settling that ought to be addressed directly and privately for everyone's sake. Otherwise, individual hearers feel that they have been "gotten," which they very often have been. While a sermon is almost always a monologue by any obvious definition, it is enhanced when the preacher understands it as part of a continuing relationship. Thus it is part of a larger dialogue, a fact which emphasizes the importance of being the same person in and out of the pulpit. Preachers for whom this is a problem, might try the relative vulnerability of preaching outside the pulpit and on the same architectural level as the hearers when circumstances permit.

The reader has probably detected repeated allusions to

New Testament epistles in this chapter. Together they form a major model of the preaching task. Through human voices, God makes an appeal, that we accept, appropriate, and develop the gift of life in Christ. Liturgy, sacraments, and preaching, are among the gifts given to help us mature in that life, and must be received and used within the body as invaluable riches, each part respecting and cherishing all the others. The overall goal is the building of a community which lives together in love, and changes the world (2 Cor. 5:20; Eph. 4:1–32).

This goal is well expressed in a collect of uncertain authorship, one which is not found in any contemporary mainstream liturgy:

> Grant we beseech thee, almighty God, unto thy Church thy Holy Spirit and the wisdom which cometh down from above, that thy word, as becometh it, may not be bound, but have free course and be preached to the joy and edifying of Christ's holy people, that in steadfast faith we may serve thee and in the confession of thy name abide unto the end; through Jesus Christ our Lord.

What binds and frees the word is our concern here. The point will not be defense of a theory of sermon building, but the exploration of ways to preach for "the joy and edifying" of Christ's people, a much higher and more rewarding goal in preaching than anything else I can imagine.

3. | Comforts

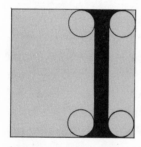

I Hate to Preach

n the first chapter the reader was asked to consider a career as a "great" preacher. Misunderstood, such a challenge can do serious damage to those who think preaching is about producing literature rather than witnessing to the power of God, or to those who think that great preaching is about being someone else, someone they cannot be. In such cases, the response to the call for renewed preaching is all too often "But I hate to preach."

Listening to people sort through the meaning of that statement once they have made it is revealing. For many, it is not the work, not the solitary hours, not the speaking in public which underlies their discomfort with preaching. Much more often there is a problem of unrealistic expectations, ill-defined greatness. Somehow people have decided that good or great preaching is sounding like old Dr. X, the rector of their parish, whose powerful and eloquent preaching was so important to their coming to faith. Or else they have decided that good preaching is witty, or poetic, or theologically profound on a level that is beyond their grasp. Still others believe that good preaching should solve people's problems and they have found to their surprise that they cannot often do that. Some have written sermons which did not seem to go over well, and find themselves afraid to "fail" again. There are also those for whom good is never good enough, who hate preaching because they do not think they will ever be excellent at it.

Surprisingly, seminaries and divinity schools have been known to offer courses in which people simply start preaching, perhaps after a few theoretical lectures, and then get buffeted about by unstructured class "discussion." Such discussion often does permanent damage to new preachers' beliefs about themselves and their abilities. The assumption of highly intuitive instructors, usually trained in another discipline, is that the sermon just gets written. I had this brought home to me by a graduate student who reported with tears of frustration that he had taken three homiletics courses, yet had never been told how to write the sermon. He had begun to suspect that there was something wrong with him.

The catalog of unhelpful perceptions is not exhausted by these examples, but the result of them all is the same: "I hate to preach." For all such people each sermon preparation becomes a threat, a debilitating experience, one to be avoided. Avoid it they do; their preaching suffers profoundly, and each sermon becomes a week of avoidance followed by a Saturday night driven by caffeine, fear, and adrenalin. My problem is that as long as preaching is perceived as a threat and occasion of probable failure, the method described in this book will go untried. So to those who hate, or to some degree fear, the task of preaching, I offer a three-part redefinition of our task. It is another way of understanding preaching, one which separates it from some of our conventional thinking, and puts "greatness" within each preacher's grasp. Again, some suggested rules.

First, What You Believe

Harry Williams, the contemporary English priest whose spiritual autobiography, *Someday I'll Find You,* is a very valuable account of the struggles the gifted undergo in the attempt to be faithful, concluded that he could no longer preach what he did not believe truly and for himself. That may appear to be a strange statement, but it contains a great truth. He is defining belief quite strictly. Williams' decision reminds us that the vocation of preaching is not about intellectually appropriating a set of things called ideas or even dogmas and then trading them in public like baseball cards or recipes, or arguing about them like politics—or religion. In such cases the contents of the Bible and the Christian faith are reduced to stock-in-trade which preachers manipulate or "apply" with the detachment and objectivity necessary to a surgeon or artillery crew.[9] "Believing" in Williams' sense, and this is also linguistically true for the ancient world in which Christianity arose, means something else. It is primarily about being in a relationship to the object of belief. Sermons whose main point is either to prove or disprove the historical fact of Jesus' resurrection are a case in point. They seldom avoid being

---

[9] This is not an entirely modern problem. In 1609 John Donne complained that "the divines of these times" had become like lawyers, who are capable of arguing a position without personal investment: "That for which they plead is none of theirs. They write for Religion without it" (Letter to Henry Goodyear).

"head trips," intellectual journeys whose appeal is largely limited to the speaker. On the other hand, consider sermons whose main point is to relate what Christians, including the preacher, know of the power and presence of the resurrected Christ and which then invite others to share that experience. They give authentic witness. More important, they move us who hear the sermon to a vital issue: will I seek to know and follow the resurrected Christ as Lord in a wonderfully transformed way of living?

Sermons which cleverly explicate deep doctrines which are not part of the preacher's own experience of faith may entertain and inform, but seldom do they inspire, and almost never do they ring true. Wilfred Owen wrote letters and verse in the trenches of World War I, and the reader may be familiar with those of his war poems set to music in Benjamin Britten's *War Requiem*. Although Owen's faith was tested by much of the war's horrors, it was shaken more by Christians, especially the "pulpit professionals," as he put it, who commented on the issues of the conflict from the security of England. Owen's disgust proceeded from their treating war as though it were either a sporting event or an idea to be analyzed with no serious thought given to the blood and agony it entailed.[10] Owen was not requiring every preacher to experience the slime of the trenches first-hand, but he did require every preacher to find out something of what it was like, of what the real issues were, before saying so much as a word. If that is the bad news, the good news is that preachers who do limit themselves to preaching what they know

---

[10] See Wilfred Owen, *Collected Letters* (London: Oxford, 1967), passim. By August of 1917 Owen had concluded that "there are no more Christians at the present moment than there were at the end of the first century." Some historians believe that the British general staff went on for at least half of the war using metaphors drawn primarily from the playing fields. The horrors of trench and gas warfare only slowly changed their language patterns.

(including what they know they do not know), seldom have to worry about authenticity or directness, and seldom have to worry about keeping the attention of their audience.

Beyond that, this principle keeps the preacher's soul intact, safe from the very real and very damning sins of the intellect. Preaching is a business about words, and as we become good preachers we come to love words and their power, their subtlety. That love can take us beyond what we have any business saying. C. S. Lewis' *The Great Divorce* lays the trap out well. In the very pit of hell Lewis places a theological debating society, so caught up in its rhetoric it is unaware of its damnation. To rub it in, Lewis introduces us to a bishop about to deliver a paper on how Jesus' career would have progressed if he had matured a bit and developed a better attitude toward authority. After that light twitting of the episcopal mindset, Lewis returns to dead earnest, and later in the book concludes: "Every poet and musician and artist, but for Grace, is drawn away from the love of the thing he tells to the love of telling it, till, down in Deep Hell, they cannot be interested in God at all, but only in what they say about him."[11]

So for everyone's sake, not least our own, the first rule is that we must preach what we believe, the truths in relation to which we live. Does this rule limit the preacher? It certainly does: on the surface level, there is no reason to believe that each pulpit can or should be an authority on every topic from archaeology to zoology. Furthermore, one's faith does not give one automatic authority to pronounce on politics, economics, or the personal problems which trouble so many. If we are going to talk about issues, *as indeed we should,* we need first to understand and be involved in them intellectually and spiritually. There are limits

---

[11] C.S. Lewis, *The Great Divorce*, (New York: Macmillan, 1974), p. 81.

to what each of us is capable of grasping, of course, and there are times when the responsible thing is to say "I'm not in a position to preach about this." If I believe that I should be in a position to preach on it, however, I need to get into contact with what is at stake, and that may mean deliberately going on personal journeys, becoming deliberately troubled by the issues about which I believe the church needs to hear. Simply reading an article in either *The National Review* or *The Nation* does not qualify as wrestling spiritually with an issue, but that reading may indeed stimulate it.

Perhaps more importantly, this rule provides an effective editorial check on the sermon. I have found that whenever I am experiencing the joy (or even exaltation) of writing what seems to be a brilliant insight or just the right answer for some issue in a sermon and want to charge right on to illustrate that point, I must pull back and ask, "Do I *believe* this? How do I *know* it?" "Have I ever carried the weight of the burden I am binding?" For me at least, if the answer to the first two is unclear, or if to the third question it is anything other than unqualified "yes," I must start that section over. Such questions take much of the surface joy out of sermon writing, of course: there can be no "gotcha's" in a sermon the way there can be in letters to the editor. These questions also naturally empower preaching by driving the preacher to a much deeper level where he or she must engage truly an aspect of faith before proclaiming it. If a "truth" proclaimed is personally important to the preacher, it probably will be just as important to the hearer. Even sermons whose message is "I don't have the last word on this but here is where I am in my struggle with it" can ring with the authority of the Christian soul truly engaged in the effort to be faithful, and thus they have important effect on the efforts of others. People are encouraged to take up the struggle themselves, and are also shown that it is possible not to have the answers and still thrive spiritually.

Rule Two: Comforts

This brings us to the second rule, one related to the first. As mentioned previously, George Herbert describes his country parson as preparing sermons by laboring over the scriptures, which he called "the storehouse and magazine of comfort," and then patristic writers, and modern commentators, and finally sharing the "comforts" he found with the congregation. That is all. Anybody can put together a tirade diagnosing the faults of society or the congregation. This "bad news" is the easiest part of a sermon to write. However, the harder questions remain. What makes our situation bearable, our tasks possible, our new life available? St. Paul unblushingly refers in his writing to "my gospel," a concept dealt with below in Chapter Seven, and the New Testament makes clear that what Paul emphasized about the faith in his preaching was not the same as what John found it important to express. How do you put together and express what you believe? What do you as preacher find in the scriptures, the tradition and the life of the contemporary church that in fact helps *you* with the issues of our Christian call, our life and discipleship? When you asked yourself if you believed your flashes of insight, how did you know? What stories and images came to mind? Preachers do not have to search homiletical magazines to find the core of a sermon when they follow the model Herbert lays out. Rather, like the good scribe Jesus depicts, they can bring from the treasury those things both old and new which help with the issue in question. The truly exciting task of preaching is not setting other people straight; it is getting to root around in those treasures—in most cases even getting paid—to find, appropriate, and share the gifts of God. I seriously maintain that if the preacher has not yet found these gifts as they relate to the subject of the sermon, a different sermon needs to be found that week.

I am uncomfortable with sermons which every week predictably go on from a brief treatment of the text to give at length quotations from the patristic period, a modern thinker, and a portion of the liturgy: the effect is usually the same as a lecture or a preliminary study before writing a sermon: all theory and no real application. Nonetheless, an important model is given in such sermons, and one which I have found overrides my personal preferences and makes such sermons helpful for me as listener, even if on a different level than the preacher perhaps intended. The preacher in this genre over and over again gives the model of searching Bible and tradition for "comforts" to appropriate and share. Thus the first and second rules are related: intentionally limiting our preaching to what we believe commits us to making the effort to grow in faith.

Rule Three: Plain Speaking

The third rule: we are relieved from the perceived necessity for high rhetoric by remembering John Henry Newman's motto, *cor ad cor loquitur*, "heart speaks to heart." That expression has meant many things to people over the years. Here it is a reminder that what works best in sermons in our day is straightforward speaking from one Christian to another. Again, for Herbert's parson, "the character of his Sermon is holiness; he is not witty, or learned, or eloquent, but Holy. . . . [and he attains this quality by] choosing texts of Devotion, not controversy, moving and ravishing texts, whereof the Scriptures are full. Secondly, by dipping, and seasoning all our words and sentences in our hearts before they come into our mouths, with true affection, and with cordially expressing all that we say; so that the auditors may plainly perceive that every word is heart-deep."

I was once asked, disingenuously I hope, whether I thought this business of preaching from the heart means that sincerity is a good ploy, an effective pose. Far from it. If you are saying what you "believe" and emphasizing the "comforts" you have found, obscuring your message in complex packaging is simply incongruous. The nineteenth century added to our language the expression "prince of the pulpit." Such a description for powerful preaching was perhaps appropriate to an all-male presbyterate in the Gilded Age, but new occasions do in fact teach new duties. In our age "preaching" is almost completely synonymous with irrelevance, contorted phrases, condescension, or even scolding, as witness Madonna's hit, "Papa, Don't Preach." For a time like ours, the last thing that fits with the homiletical model developed here is the metaphor of a mesmerizing pulpit monarch. The congregation is seldom looking for it, and without it the preacher is freed simply to speak, to speak simply, and then gets to cherish those moments when people gratefully say: "It didn't seem like preaching; you were just talking to us." In my case the most important reinforcement I ever got was from my then ten year-old son, who remarked at lunch one Sunday, "Papa, what I like about your sermons is that you don't have to be intelligent to understand them." In both cases the point is that people who do not have to devote their minds entirely to decoding a sermon may have the energy left to hear and appropriate its content.

If being "sincere" and straightforward in what you preach still sounds like an unauthentic pose, then a few kind words are in order for posing. (Remember that here we are discussing *how*, not *what* we preach.) On a deep level we are all posing much of the time. Growing into any new role, whether that of preacher, physician, or skier, involves intentional posing.

"Posing," in this sense, is not hypocrisy. It is how, as St. Paul even said of our baptized relationship to God, we "put on" the new identity.[12] Posing may be another word to describe experientially learning the depth of what we have come to believe is true or right. Preachers have a model into which they are growing, or from which they are working. If the role choice is among pundit, Olympian deep thinker, prince of the pulpit, or pastor sincerely sharing the comforts he or she has found, I'll take the latter and work to grow into that as I learn to share what I believe. Observation suggests that this approach of choosing a model and growing into it works. Theologically we all recognize that transformation is the Spirit's business; a good deal of what this book is about is putting oneself in the place and frame of mind where that transformation can happen.

"But I've got to be me." "How can you ask me to *act* as though I'm direct and sincere?" I have a therapist friend who, when he asks people to imagine or visualize something and is told they cannot, simply says, "O.K., pretend you are visualizing . . ." If the reader wishes to speak simply and directly of what he or she believes but finds the language difficult, a little posing may be in order. Intention has more control of behavior on this level than we are sometimes prepared to admit. Keith Miller's now-classic and quite effective *Edge of Adventure* program for Christian spirituality works on the same premise: for a course period participants are to act as though Christianity were true and Christ a reality with whom they have a significant relationship. At the end of that period when intellect has been partially suspended, many are relieved to find that the relationship is real, even though they have been previously unable to think their

---

[12] This is a common expression in Pauline and deutero-Pauline material. See Romans 13:12–14; Galatians 3:27; Ephesians 4:24; 6:11–14; Colossians 3:10–14; 1 Thessalonians 5:8.

way to faith. If we wait until something becomes intellectually true for us before living in it, we may never attain it. The way to learn to speak from the heart is to intend to do so and then to speak as though from the heart about the things one believes.

Comfort and Encouragement for Preachers

Although I share these three observations to take the pressure off preachers, because they are new ideas to some people, they have occasionally backfired. Just a few days before those words were written, a student asked with a very pained look, "Don't you realize how *hard* all of this is?"

Yes, I do. I also care about that fact. When we have been socialized to have other beliefs, it is very hard for some to realize that preaching is something quite other than a religious version of public speaking. The skills for preaching discussed so far involve the basic organization of one's life, one's spirituality.

Harder still is the fact that these rules demand that the preachers who have found no resources to share now find some that they have known of personally or at least witnessed at work. A very brave student once reported that finding authentic good news, comforts, help, and direction, was so difficult for him in writing sermons that he realized that he did not believe very much, good as he was in theological studies. Thus he was suspending his seminary education for a year. During that year he was going to read and work with a spiritual director in order to grow spiritually before trying to preach any more. His solution was a rare and radical one, but it underscores the importance of the spiritual formation as an aspect of theological education. The preacher's role is only possible to the extent that he or she is living a life of prayer, reflection, and study. No one quality covers a lack of the others. For instance, reading will not substitute for reflection any more than eating builds muscle without exercise. But those hard tasks are also tremendously liberating, because they place the core of preaching in precisely what is proclaimed: God's grace and power.

In my first year out of seminary I was complaining to a senior colleague, also named Paul, at whose Minnesota church I was assisting. My complaint was that Paul and a mutual friend had such a mastery of language, such an integrity of person and sermon, such a command of the scriptures, that I felt altogether inadequate writing sermons and utterly silly when I had to preach in the presence of either of them. Paul chose not to "preach" at me in response, which would have been counter-productive and guilt-inducing in this instance. Instead he began to tell the story of his first year in parish ministry in North Dakota, working alone and in charge of two parishes. He had a few good moments, but by the end of the first year, he was mostly aware of his shortcomings and failures, which he re-counted and got my sympathy entirely. He said he had made one friend, a life-long resident of the place, and it was to this elderly farmer that he chose to unburden himself. He laid out in detail aspirations now but dimly remembered, and his perceived prob-lems and failures, which occupied most of his consciousness. The old man said nothing, just took it all in. When Paul was done, the two of them just sat for a spell.

When it came, the farmer's response was something Paul will never forget. "Why, you self-centered, whining, son-of-a-bitch—do you believe that the Lord called you?"

This is not the kind of conversation for which seminary or clinical training prepares the sensitive new cleric, then or now. Embarrassed and a little angry, Paul could barely stammer, "You know I do."

"Well, don't you think he was smart enough to know what he was getting?"

The insightful farmer was giving a message not much different from the scriptural reports of the call of reluctant prophets. Whether these passages conform to a literary form or not is irrelevant to their message, which was and is powerful.

In the narrative of his call, Isaiah protests his unworthiness and that of his people. Rather than a debate, Isaiah receives a burning coal upon his lips as outward and visible token of the interior fact that his sin is wiped away. He is freed from giving that sin further attention, and can get on with the task of speaking for Yahweh. He is then also free to respond to the question he overhears in the heavenly council: "Whom shall I send," with "Here am I; send me!" (Isaiah 6:1–8).

In another prophet's memoirs, despite the fact that the vision begins with Yahweh's announcement that he does indeed know exactly what he is getting, Jeremiah protests against his call, citing youth and ineloquence. Jeremiah's lips are also touched, but now by Yahweh's own hand, with the announcement that "I have put my words into your mouth" (Jeremiah 1:4–10). Jeremiah is later to find that those words are not the easiest to digest, but his vision at this early stage was one which freed him to speak.

Moral worthiness, years of experience, and rhetorical talent are not the homiletical qualifications underscored in these biblical accounts. Both Isaiah and Jeremiah have authority because of a transforming experience of God. If preaching is a vocation, God is to be understood as author of the call and source of the words which are about or which are themselves the gifts to be shared in preaching. "Command what you will, but give what you command," was Augustine's prayer. Contemporary ordination rites take a sense of personal call quite seriously. Those of the Book of Common Prayer, for example, have the bishop ask the candidates for each of the three orders of ministry, whether they believe that they "are truly called by God."

What would be the result of a follow-up question asking whether the candidate believes that God knows precisely the character of the one called and is willing to work with it?

That we come to depend on a relationship with God to make preaching a bearable vocation, provides the preacher's basic congruence. As Dean Alan Jones has pointed out, everyone is a word in flesh, a message. For those whose task in the church is the stewardship of words, this seems a particularly important observation. The three rules and the story of the farmer and young preacher add up to one thing in this regard. The words we speak and the "word" we are need to be, and can be, very nearly the same. The joy of preaching is that those who hear the command to preach are over and over again invited into the process of discovering what is in fact richly given.

PART TWO:

Preparation and Delivery

4. Starting Out: Workspace and Mindset

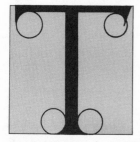

This second part describes the process of writing sermons. Preparation is first of all preparation of the preacher. Thus in this chapter two kinds of temporal "workshops" are set up in the preacher's mind. From there consideration turns to the mindset of the preacher upon sitting down to prepare, and the relationship of preaching to other liturgical actions as they shape the preacher's attitude. Classical manuals of pastoral theology termed the kind of issues addressed here as part of the preacher's *habitus practicus*, an antique phrase designating the internal state and set of attitudes which are necessary to do the pastoral task well.

It must be emphasized again that there are many models for sermons, and that ultimately each one of us develops a personal process (or several) for writing sermons. This chapter and the one which follows provide one way to start, one which has at least been road-tested. It is a programmed engagement with scripture, the church year, self, and those for whom we preach. However, the first thing the preacher needs is a mental workspace, time carved out for preparation.

Finding the Time

Everybody has too much to do.

That is a fact of life, and each of us responds to that painful fact in different ways. One unhealthy response is to try to do everything, becoming a compulsive worker, with dangerous consequences for personal and family health.

The healthier strategy is to assign priorities to tasks and manage time accordingly. Otherwise one simply gets lost in the sea of worthwhile possibilities through which we all sail, or else becomes immobilized in the seaweed of phone calls, administrative details, junk mail and unproductive meetings. None of those seaweed items can be avoided completely, but the amount of time they receive must be controlled.

Sermons require time, and they will not get written if time is not planned for them, especially if the truth is that one would rather avoid preparing them altogether. The first block of time, those twenty or thirty minutes which get the sermon started, needs to be as early in the week as possible. John Donne started on Sunday night. Many of us would prefer Monday morning. Intuitives need time to explore and test their visions, while sensates will want time to get to the depth of the data and begin to arrange it.

Those twenty to thirty minutes are harder to find than might be expected. The problem is that there is always something else to do, and often that something else seems to have more immediacy about its demand than preparing a sermon which will not have to be preached for six or seven days.

Finding the time, both to begin and also to complete a

sermon, has come to mean two things for me. The first is the skill of "chunking down," as some experts call it. Many people lose a lot of time by a false logic erected on one truth. "I only have forty-five minutes right now, and I can't do that project in less than six hours. . . ." The only truths in that statement are that I have forty-five minutes, and that six hours are longer than the forty-five minutes at hand. The false logic is that because I only have this little space of time right now, all I can do is to "kill" it and wait for a big piece of "quality time." The fact is that we have very few uninterrupted four- or six-hour blocks in the week, but we do have many blocks of an hour or less. Chunking down in this instance means taking big tasks, such as writing sermons, and breaking them down into small chunks, tasks which can be done in the kind of time one actually has. Thus the process described in this chapter is already broken down into at least seven steps, each one of which can be subdivided if necessary.

Chunking down reminds us of another reality: all those half- and three quarter-hours add up. They are tremendous resources, to be used intentionally. "Killing time" as an expression is intriguing: what one is actually doing is wasting a non-retrievable part of one's life, so the killing is in one sense far from metaphorical.

This brings us to the second aspect of finding the time: strengthening our ability to set priorities, especially for the longer times needed for writing and revision. What are your major goals for ministry? What are your parish's major needs of you? The answers to questions like these are starting points for setting personal goals and establishing priorities. It is to priority work, into which category sermon writing, parish visitation, and pastoral counselling fall for most of us, that we best devote our high-energy productive time. Defining that time may take some reflection and keeping track. My own conclusions are fairly typical. Like many of my colleagues, I find that I write best in the early morning when I am freshest, and have energy to tackle challenging interpersonal encounters in the early afternoon or early evening when I have been somewhat renewed. Thus the low-energy times of late morning and late afternoon become the best time for me to handle administrative detail, the mail, and routine meetings and appointments. Your pattern may be very different: the point is that becoming aware of the pattern and planning for it provide a very effective way of finding time for the longer parts of sermon writing. There are indeed emergencies which interrupt the schedule, but even in large parishes there are not so many of them that a general pattern cannot be maintained.

Much of our day is perforce taken up with the minor details, the administrative "seaweed" mentioned above. These things are often quite secondary to our main goals in ministry, but they have to be done. Consequently, they should be relegated to the low-energy parts of the day, whenever those parts occur for an individual. With difficulty I have had to learn that the mail really can sit there until 4:30, and that the desk drawer will not need cleaning if I do not shove things into it in the first place. Non-essential phone messages can be responded to at a time you choose, within the limits of civility.

All of the above is to say that the many small or interior bits of sermon preparation can happen in short periods of time. The longer periods, the time needed for writing and revision, have to be planned for, and the time devoted to them protected.

But I'm a people person. This seems to be an important objection to organizing and protecting sermon time, as many preachers are in fact highly extroverted, and are energized by their contacts with others. It is important for them to remember that it is the sermon that is their principal contact with the largest number of people during the week, and their only contact with most of them. Understood that way, preparation for preaching to all those people becomes something precious to "people" persons, something to which they are likely to want to devote carefully planned time, and experience preparation as a kind of encounter with all those people. That said, I must admit that I have also found it helpful at times to visualize myself chained to my desk until the task was done.

Starting Out

There is a pronounced hesitancy in general treatments of preaching to own up to what the truly effective preachers I have known readily admit. The entire process of sermon preparation is experienced differently when begun with prayer and then pursued as a kind of prayer itself. It was not an easy decision to put that thought into writing in an age when homiletics books often have become as technical and unfeeling as sex manuals, but there it is.[13] The previous chapter urges a self-understanding for preachers which arises from their relationship to God, and here they are asked to bring that relationship into direct consciousness when entering sermon preparation. It seems to be a rule that preachers cannot simultaneously demonstrate how clever they are, and how powerful God is to save. The sermon will do one job or the other, and prayer may make the difference in determining which job is done. The style of constant prayer which Brother Lawrence called the "practice of the presence of God," has particular relevance to the homiletical task for those

---

[13] A review article in the professional journal for the teaching of preaching places recourse to prayer in sermon preparation into the category of "cliched" advice, bearable only among those who have "no access to any rhetorical theory." *Homiletic*, Vol. XV. No. 2 (Winter, 1990), p. 26

who would preach truly. This constant paying attention to our relationship to God is, after all, a principle expression of the gospel we preach. From another point of view, if any of what Chapter Three asserts is true, it simply makes good sense to take advantage of it: the pressure really does come off and creativity occurs more readily when preaching comes from relationship with God.

Fairly obviously, the preacher who prays in beginning to prepare would first of all simply be in the presence of God, and then might rightly ask various gifts of discernment, concentration, and perseverance. However, the prayer can go to another level. It has become something of a commonplace to observe that the hardest but most important prayer of all is "God, I put myself at your disposal." When that prayer ends with "and particularly in this sermon," the religious public speaker begins to become a preacher. Such a prayer orients all the homiletical efforts towards a doing of God's will in a given place at a given time, which the preacher often finds means quite the opposite of ventilating what one feels strongly about at the moment. Such a prayer also puts one in a place where preparing sermons can bring the soul of the preacher moments of surprise and delight.

If the entire sermon process is begun with a prayer and continued as a prayer, its results will reflect that. For instance, as one who has wrestled with the temptations of language and often lost, I have come to learn that while one can imagine jokes written in prayer, it is hard to imagine the prayer experience producing words which belittle, manipulate, or give false comfort.

Having placed the sermon in the arena of prayer, I find it helpful to do two more acts of recollection before tackling the biblical texts. These involve considering the liturgy of the day and the function of that day's lectionary in the church year. If these are considered only after the texts are studied, it may be too late, and then the sermon must be bent or hammered to fit the occasion for which it was ostensibly prepared.

The Function of the Liturgy In Sermon Preparation

Part One made two principal points about the sermon in the liturgy. The sermon itself is a liturgical act, and thus has ritual significance: its existence gives expression to our belief that there is a present-day word of the Lord. The sermon relates a message from the day's scriptures in such a way as to inform and direct the offering of ourselves symbolically in the liturgy and actively in our lives.

What else does the liturgy contribute to the mindset of the preacher as sermon preparation begins?

First of all, "liturgy" means something much more important than "what the people do." It seems that in the 1960s this possibly solipsistic and surely self-indulgent definition enabled some liturgical experimenters to say that because the liturgy was whatever happened in church, any worship forms they themselves staged were beyond criticism. They arrived at this peculiar definition from a too casual observation of liturgy's Greek roots, however. The first of the two components of the word is indeed "work." However, the second is "for the public" *(leïtos),* not "the people" *(laos).* The word "liturgy" in the ancient world was not employed to mean what the people did: in that case it could have just as easily meant starving or rioting in the street. No, the word's actual use in the pre- and non-Christian world was more along the lines of "public work," "public service," something "done for the good of all." From this a secondary religious sense of "service to the gods for the sake of the people" evolved. Hellenistic Judaism picked up the word in this religious sense of worship conducted for the public good, and this is the origin of the Christian use. The daily secular use survived, however, and was a word for all manner of events staged for the public; even some entertainments could be called "liturgy" because they were understood to contribute to the welfare of the community. This is precisely what John Chrysostom means when he calls his preaching "my liturgy." He understood preaching as his contribution offered to God for the common good of the assembled Christian people. Thus while we as a church affirm that in the liturgy each member of the assembly participates in all appropriate ways, this does not permit us to think of liturgy as a forum for self-expression for its own sake. The implication of this truth for our preaching is that from the first moment of preparation the sermon must in *intention* be not for the preacher or a small constituency, but for the good of the entire assembly. This becomes one of the most demanding aspects of sermon preparation. It is also a place where we encounter the living truth of the axiom *lex orandi legem statuat credendi,* the rule of prayer constitutes or founds the rule of belief.[14]

Furthermore, it should be clear at this point that the much-discussed "relationship" between preaching and worship simply is not a problem. As Paul Scherer once put it, preaching "does not go hand in hand with worship or break in on it for a while. . . . It occasions worship. . . . Show God to your people and they will worship."[15] R.E.C. Brown has put it more simply, in finding it an essential part of the apologetic task "to stimulate wonder."[16]

---

[14] The best in-depth word study of *leitourgia* and related words is that found under *leitourgeo* in G. Kittel, ed., *Theological Dictionary of the New Testament,* Vol. IV (Grand Rapids: Wm. B. Eerdmans, 1967), pp. 215–231.

[15] Paul Scherer, *For We Have This Treasure* (New York: Harper & Row, 1944), p. 13.

[16] R. E. C. Browne, *The Ministry of the Word* (Philadelphia: Fortress, 1976), p. 119.

Beyond this, however, when it is working well, liturgy is life and death business, bringing us to the very brink of non-being, and in the face of death itself to the celebration of new life.[17] Those two aspects of the celebration need each other. In the broadest sense there are no surprise endings in liturgy. It is the victory of Christ that we celebrate and appropriate in worship that creates the context in which we preachers treat the great issues, many of which are otherwise unbearable or overwhelming. On the other hand, without any exploration of the real issues of life, the "hard questions," the mystery of faith degenerates into a security blanket or worse, pious escapism from the challenges and joys of discipleship.

Thus the sermon must be congruent with its setting. It is important that the sermon address significant issues in a significant way because it is part of a liturgy which is the meeting of God and the church, a liturgy in which the church is constituted anew. For example, like the liturgy, the sermon may say hard things, pronounce judgments, make demands. But those things are said to people who will also hear words of absolution, share the peace of the Lord, and together give thanks that "you have delivered us from evil, and made us worthy to stand before you."[18] And most compelling of all, in most situations the preacher must preach knowing that he or she will also in a very few minutes be sharing sacred food with those to whom the sermon was addressed. The sum of this celebration of word and sacrament is to be God's expected answer to the prayer, "now send us out to do the work you have given us to do." Sermons need to be prepared with that context in mind (al-

---

[17] In this regard, see especially Aidan Kavanagh, *On Liturgical Theology.* (New York: Pueblo, 1984).

[18] These words of Hippolytus (ca. 215) are echoed in contemporary Lutheran, Roman Catholic, and Anglican eucharistic liturgies, among others.

though the context need not be specifically addressed very often), so that the hard or challenging things in sermons always occur in relationship to the power of God to grow, endure, and triumph, and in the context of our relationship to each other as baptized brothers and sisters about to share the great meal. I shall argue later that this liturgical principle needs to control the proportions of the "good news" and "bad news" in sermons. What it means here is that the preacher consciously begins work in a relationship to the members of the assembly that must be described in words much like "nurture," "community," and "love."

Rhetorical technique must be examined in the light of the liturgy just as much as content is scrutinized. For example, consider the homiletical function of humor, which I mentioned in the discussion of prayer in the previous section. There has been a great deal of laughing in church in the last decades, and in many places there is a fairly strong expectation that sermons have funny bits. That is not entirely inappropriate. Humor can have many salutary functions, functions which are congruent with the liturgy. It certainly gets attention, and in some cases builds rapport quickly. Humor also gives permission to name horrors we would otherwise ignore. It cuts problems down to a size which we can endure to examine in public. Humor is also a way of saying that we are in this together. Furthermore, in the Biblical and patristic traditions it is also a tool for deriding our old enemies, particularly sin and death.

Unfortunately, humor can also be a tool for keeping ourselves at a distance from the subject at hand. It can give the impression that we are not taking that subject seriously. Overused, especially when its function is to mask the anxiety of the speaker, humor trivializes the subject and the occasion to a point which comes close to insulting the audience. Finally, if humor is used in such a way as to blunt the edge of the liturgy's encounter with God, in effect to domesticate the Almighty, it has gone too far. Thus like all rhetorical devices, it is used with care, used in a way appropriate to the sermon's place in the liturgy.

Finally, liturgy controls the personal element in preaching. Like John Donne, most of us feel free to use first person pronouns in sermons. However, when we examine Donne's sermons, his use of "I" is always one that invites, one that includes the audience. His is the "I" of universal experience or hope, and does not focus the listener's attention on Donne's soul in particular. First person encounter is shared only to the extent that it offers a connection for the listener to the point being made about human experience. It is appropriate to the kind of corporate experience liturgy is meant to be. Liturgy fails when it becomes "Mother Smith's mass," and the sermon in the liturgy just as surely fails when worshippers remember most, "Father Smith sure felt bad when his Volvo ran over that kitten." This is a point to which we shall have to return, but here it illustrates a constraint that the liturgy puts on the sermon. That constraint has a very positive effect: it keeps the sermon relevant in the best sense by keeping its focus on that with which most of the hearers can identify, on that to which we are all called. To get ready to preach in the liturgy is to prepare to be an instrument, a part of what is bigger than any one person present, but vital to every individual.

Biblical Preaching in a Liturgical Year

The preacher is about to work with biblical texts. What makes a sermon biblical? This is not an easy question in a day when the preacher cannot assume a great deal of biblical knowledge on the part of the hearers. There is a strong temptation to overcome that lack of biblical knowledge by regularly converting the sermon into a miniature Christian education hour, in which one or all the lessons are explained in detail in the effort to overcome biblical illiteracy. One can sympathize quite deeply with the urge to get people to know the Bible. However, as we have defined the sermon and its function, that sort of preaching cannot be the weekly norm, and certainly the liturgical celebration rules out academic verse-by-verse exposition on any regular basis. In *The Country Parson*, George Herbert objected to "crumbling a text into small parts" because such a method "hath neither in it sweetness, nor gravity, nor variety, since the words apart are not scripture, but a dictionary." Our concern here is to build a sermon which has a point, a main idea, and that goal rules out an unfocussed collection of observations about the three lessons or even about one of them. There are many ways to study the scriptures, and most of them, including sequential exposition, are better done in an educational forum, rather than the sermon in the liturgy. The tradition of the sermon at the end of Evening Prayer might well be revived to accommodate a more academic or didactic kind of preaching, and no apology needs to be made for reinvigorating our efforts at programs of adult education.

Nevertheless, good preaching within the model proposed here should certainly increase in people an understanding of the text and also the desire to know more about the contents of the Bible. This is so because the liturgical sermon gets its biblical character from the fact that it applies a message in the day's scriptures to the life of the assembly, and hearers thus experience the Bible as essential resource. Hearers should want to know more. The sermon intentionally gives the hearer insight both into the central core of meaning in the text(s), and also connects that core to our Christian life. It means that despite the cautions just suggested about overly expository preaching, the text is dealt with so that the listener both feels its force and understands why it is important for what the preacher is saying. This means that preaching is *not* biblical when a text is read and immediately abandoned for a reminiscence: "this passage reminds me of the time . . ." or when one of the day's readings finally appears at the end of the sermon only as an illustration of the preacher's real point, one foreign to the text. At the very least we come to the scriptures each week expecting to find in them a word from God which has some use for those seeking to be Christ's people. Thus biblical preaching is preaching that takes seriously a message of the week's scriptures and puts that message into contact with our lives as followers of Jesus. The hallmark of biblical preaching is the fact that what is preached is determined by the content of the text. Leander Keck has observed that our biblical illiteracy problem is not helped by the kind of preaching which starts by quoting a verse from one of the pericopes and then goes on to say something which "could have been suggested just as well by a fortune cookie."[19] In Keck's model, preaching is biblical when the sermon has the same function as the text. There certainly are times when each of us needs to say things other than those pointed out in the lessons for the day, and I have no quarrel with that: norms are not unbending requirements. Nevertheless, we need to keep in mind that sermons of that kind are something other than biblical preaching as it is usually defined, lest we think we are doing the job of proclaiming the scriptures when in fact we are not.

The steps proposed in the next chapter ask the preacher to wrestle with the scriptural message as it stands and to preach primarily out of that encounter. I suggest that while we are searching the scriptures, we also allow them to search us,

---

[19] Leander E. Keck. *The Bible in the Pulpit.* Nashville: Abingdon, 1978, p. 101.

and on their own terms. With that in mind, the last part of the mindset we are discussing involves the lectionary and liturgical year.

Liturgy will not let us alone. It imposes its disciplines that we might grow into the full stature of Christ, becoming fully human and even divine. Thus like Christianity itself, liturgy calls introverts into community and asks extroverts to contemplate. It also asks each of us to appropriate a full, a complete gospel: neither spiritual nor social theology is enough by itself. Liturgy's chief discipline for this kind of formation is the cycle of the liturgical year with its observances and lectionary. What we do, what we hear, see and say through this cycle is meant to shape us as those in whom God's purposes are being worked out. The year also assumes that each of us is "in process," that we do not graduate. Thus there will be Lent again this year precisely because I did not get all good last year. There will be Easter again because I still must be about the business of encountering the resurrected Christ and coming to know freedom and power as I live in his life. *The fact that I already know the story is not the point*; the emphasis is on incorporating it into my being. It is here that the liturgy does indeed ask all the people to work all of the time. Thus the Bible is explored without the objectivity of someone who merely wants to know what is in it. It is rather poured over by those who want to know what is in it for them as they are formed by the Spirit at this time in our corporate life. The preacher in this setting begins by asking "What time is it?"

This is to say that there is a discernible hermeneutic at work in existence of the lectionary, one which is of greatest significance to preachers' attitude toward their work. That hermeneutic is fundamentally ecclesial and communal. The place of the lectionary within the liturgical cycle leads us to conclude that the Protestant formula, that the Bible creates the church, is inaccurate and unhelpful on the primary level. Just as surely the feeling of some of the more catholic Christians that scripture and liturgy are antagonists is unfounded. The scriptures of both Israel and Christianity arose in the setting of an already worshipping and witnessing community, one already created by the action of God. This is, of course, why communities which work backwards and try to "base worship on the Bible" end up with less than satisfying worship patterns and inevitably go on to develop their own rituals, all the while insisting that they have none. The church and its worship are scripture's home, and the matrix in which it arose, not its creation or its enemy. The system by which the church appropriates its scriptural treasures is the lectionary. In it lessons are grouped in ways which allow them to enrich and instruct the liturgical process and appropriate the power of the great mysteries from Advent until Pentecost. The lectionary has another mission: throughout the year, and especially on "green" Sundays after Epiphany and Pentecost, it puts us in touch with a very wide range of scriptural content, so that Christ's people become mature, complete, equipped for every good work. The built-in hermeneutic is that these lessons, in this order, and at this time, are read because they have something to say to our corporate experience of Christian development. Thus biblical preaching in the liturgical context means that what is preached is determined by the content of the text, particularly as that text applies to the day's observance. Hence we begin by asking what time it is.

Liturgical time is first of all experienced as a tension between the week and the year. The fundamental observance is Sunday, the first day of the week, our day to celebrate the resurrection. It came to be spoken of as the Eighth Day, the beginning of eschatological hope. For the early Christians the resurrection celebration was much more than an equivalent of the Sabbath (many of them still observed that day without much alteration). Sunday celebrated the resurrection disturbance and redirection of history, not completion and rest. Thus, no matter how much we come to Sunday services for moments of peace and for time with God—and they are indeed provided—we are also present *expecting something to happen.* "Finish then thy new creation" is an essential part of the homiletical expectation: the preacher and congregation approach the scriptures expecting God to be at work among, in, and through them. They come expecting to have the status quo disturbed, just as it was at the first Easter. The preacher begins work expecting to change personally from the encounter. If that is not the case, it is likely that the end result will be of diminished value.

Sundays are linked together into a year. The cycle of time in a liturgical year gathers us to a time of the ancestors, to the events that flowed to and from the events of the first Easter. We are never alone when we preach, we are connected to the generations of the faithful and to Christ's resurrection. That paschal celebration itself is the center of the Christian year. Everything in the sermon proceeds from the belief that because Christ lives I too shall live . . . even now. The victory is won; the tricky bit is appropriating that victory. That is a primary homiletical task. The preacher begins work expecting that no matter how painful the process of growth may be, we survive the pain and joy breaks through.

Feasts of the incarnation and the coming of the Spirit, Christmas and Pentecost, important as they are, were added later than the paschal celebration, and must be linked to it. There is in later Anglican theology a clear emphasis on the incarnation, while in Roman Catholic and Lutheran discourse the cross receives more notice. However, neither approach makes much sense without the resurrection. The centrality of the resurrection and flow of the church year saves preachers from having to emphasize one at the expense of the other. The Christmas–Epiphany cycle gives us a vision of the Word being made flesh and dwelling among us. Christ's presence shows us both God's nature and our own. Lent and Holy Week give us the opportunity to explore and strengthen our own love as we enter the dessert and then follow Jesus to the cross. It is precisely there that the incarnation makes its biggest impact: God-with-us remains faithful to us even unto death at our hands. What the Easter and its great fifty days celebrate is the triumph of that incarnate-crucified word from God, and the truth of our already being vindicated as we walk in newness of life. Preachers are most effective when they gauge where the community is in this progression from Advent preparation to Pentecost celebration and allow that assessment actually to set the stage for the reception of the scriptures.

Most of us who have struggled to find the "theme" of the day's lessons have occasionally concluded that lectionary committees were mad or else a thousand times too subtle for mere mortals in the pulpit. There is relief from the frustration that accompanies such a view. In a primary sense, *the lessons do not supply the theme: the year does.* The frustration is relieved when the lectionary is seen as partner with the collect of the day, preface, and overall liturgy. The question then becomes, what do these lessons say to us at this point in our liturgical cycle? Put another way, the lectionary is not a burden imposed on the preacher to limit creativity, but rather an intricate part of the liturgical and homiletical package which is our concern as we gather for worship, and which sets the stage for creativity and variety. Particularly in the Advent through Pentecost Sundays, the preacher approaches the lectionary texts expecting to find connections to the day's liturgy and the Church's movement through the liturgical cycle.[20] This is so because liturgical time

---

[20] Those readers who wish to explore the theoretical underpinnings of the liturgical year should consult Adrian Nocent, *The Liturgical Year*, (Collegeville: Liturgical Press, 1977). Nocent also provides valuable "biblical-liturgical re-

and its lectionary represent a special kind of remembering. They are not as much commemoration as they are anamnesis. Each term needs explanation.

Consider commemoration first; it has its place, to be sure. We do need to remember our roots, need to stand again in Joseph's lovely garden, need to watch once more as the lions attack the martyrs, need to meet the members of the great cloud of witnesses. We are a generation which needs more than many to reestablish our roots in the past, lest our spiritual energy be further squandered on reinventing the wheel. Thus there is a great deal to be said for looking at the Church's family album, so to speak, or at Egeria's "slides" of her fourth century trip to the holy land.

Commemoration's appeal can degenerate into the largely historical and even sentimental, into that nostalgic impotence that Marianne Micks has called the "tourist" view of the tradition.[21] It is thus helpful to remember that although commemoration itself does need to take place, we are much of the time after a bigger kind a remembering, what students of liturgy have come to call "anamnesis." Anamnesis is that lively contact with the past that appropriates its effects in the present. Simply put, the answer to "why is this night different from all other nights?" is that *"tonight* the Lord brought *us* from captivity into freedom."* The children who ask that question at Passover learn to experience their personal history in a new way as it meets the still-active past. For Christians, the liturgical year and its preach-

---

flections" which bring together exegetical and liturgical concerns in an exemplary way. Those who wish to expand their understanding of the relationship of lectionary to liturgy on a Sunday-by-Sunday basis may wish to consult the *Lectionary Preaching Workbook* George M. Bass has produced for C.S.S. Press of Lima, Ohio. Volumes of this project (still in process) are available in a number of series for each of cycle of the three-year lectionary.

21 See Marianne Micks, *The Future Present* (New York: Seabury, 1970).

ing are anamnesis in the same way that the great sacraments of baptism and eucharist are: the effect of what was done in the past is available to us as present reality, and we are grafted into the history that is re-called in the rite today. As the Exodus becomes real for that child at the Passover seder, Christ's passage through death to life becomes the dynamic core of the Christian's identity today through that faithful act called anamnesis.

What is less readily grasped is the fact that like the sacraments, liturgical preaching from this view of history also "remembers" the future, a concept to which we shall return in Chapter Seven. What we expect the future to bring controls our present behavior to a great degree. How our corporate anticipation of God's future shapes our individual beliefs about our own futures is as important a part of preaching as it is of our praying. The rigorous journey on which the gospel calls us to set out makes sense only because it is promised that we shall arrive. We sit down to begin sermons believing that it is all far from being in vain, that God's reign will come, and that we are seeking to clear the path for it. And so to work.

5. From Text to Main Idea

t last we come to the point where the actual study of scripture and the rest of the liturgical material is addressed. Through seven steps a Main Idea for the sermon can arise. The Main Idea is the "objective" mentioned in the second chapter, and is the organizing principle for the content of the sermon. Of the many good ideas which emerge from the preacher's study, it is the one chosen to be the point of the sermon, the concept which the preacher intends for the hearers to take home with them knowing to some degree how to use in their lives. Sermons which have a functioning central idea do not leave hearers wondering what "all that" was about, or wishing, as an exasperated friend put it to me when he learned that I was going off to seminary, that we preachers would "make your point and shut up." He and I are still in touch, and still talk about preaching. What I have come to realize in our continuing conversations is that what makes sermons seem interminable to him, as to so many others, is lack

of focus, a sense of one unrelated idea coming after another with no end in sight. Time is not really the issue when the hearers have some idea of where they are being taken. So the Main Idea serves the preacher by providing unity and control over content, and serves the hearer by providing cohesion and increased intelligibility.

A *caveat:* The Main Idea concept is not about controlling the hearer, nor is the sermon an exercise in brain washing. People can and do hear many profitable things in and through sermons, things which the preacher may not have intended. That fact does not legitimate a scatter gun or casual approach to homiletics, however.

The Main Idea emerges for some preachers by amassing and then narrowing data, and for others by reflecting on the already-studied material, consciously or not, until "aha" comes. Whether one needs the time for "aha" to jell or needs time to sort through the learnings and observations, it is best to start early in the week, certainly no later than Monday night. There is a special word in this to intuitives and to those who "work best under pressure," and more especially to those who as a rule work *only* when under pressure. The faster and better your mind works, the more refined and matured will be the sermon that is begun early in the week, even if nothing is written down until later.

It is said that a student once approached Rabbi Abraham Heschel with excitement and pride, and announced that he had finally "been through the Talmud." In reply Heschel asked, "But has the Talmud been through you?" Similarly, George Herbert advised that those preparing for ministry ought "not to think, that when they read the Fathers, or Schoolmen, a Minister is made and the thing done. The greatest and hardest preparation is within." What follows is an attempt to insure that in order for us to preach authentically, the scriptures get to go through us. They cannot do that at the last minute on a Saturday night. Like the rabbinical student and the Talmud, in relationship to the scriptures we preach what has been through us. Certainly our preaching begins with exegesis, and just as certainly we do not preach the technical findings of exegesis, which are but a first step. Exegesis means, quite literally, the "leading out" of the meaning of the text, particularly the meaning it had at the moment it was set down. It is in lively encounter with that meaning that the sermon usually emerges, and it is that encounter which we seek here to cultivate.

This is the hard way to write sermons, as Herbert intimates. It means that the preacher is choosing to become personally vulnerable at every step of preparation. The preacher is starting early enough in the week to have to live with the scripture to be proclaimed, to worry about it and be worried by it. This may be the method's chief use: it produces sermons which mean something to the preacher and which may also use his or her pain and joy as source of deep insight.

What follows is presented in *steps* which some people do sequentially and discretely, and which others do in a different way without particular awareness of doing separate tasks. It is assumed that the preacher enters upon them having done the spiritual, liturgical, and lectionary preparation of mind and heart described in the previous chapter. That is, the steps assume that the preacher is practicing the presence of God, is aware of preparing to preach in and for the Christian assembly, and knows what time it is, liturgically speaking. There is no reason why much of what is described in these steps cannot be done with other people, especially a group of preachers who have established some trust. I have also enjoyed presenting my preliminary findings to a Wednesday morning Bible class and being stimulated and sometimes corrected by their insights, questions, illustrations, and shared experiences.

5. From Text to Main Idea   **83**

My preference is to do Steps One through six on Monday, and then to give myself a long time to think over the results and come to a Main Idea (Step Seven). Others will want to allocate time in accordance with how they function best.

Step One. Read all of the lessons and the psalm over a few times. If you know other languages well enough, even modern languages, try reading the scriptures in them too, but nothing technical is necessarily happening here. Here we are taking the time to fill the mind, to become acquainted with the territory we will help others explore.

Step Two. What are you bringing to the texts? The late Rachel Hosmer insisted that before they begin exegetical work, it is important for preachers and other students of the Bible to consider their immediate and personal reactions to the words before them. In preparing sermons I find that her idea is of great help, and suggest some questions for preachers to ask themselves. "What do I hope the text means?" "What am I afraid it might mean?" "What issues in my life and ministry suggest themselves?" "What memories or hurts does it stir up?" "Which of my beliefs or even prejudices does it seem to confirm or attack?"

The importance of Step Two cannot be over emphasized. When this step is not taken, it is quite likely that the sermon will go wrong. Not taking this introspective step ranks right next to failing to have a Main Idea, as the chief cause of sermons ostensibly about one thing being disturbed by the appearance of agendas, often destructive ones, in places where they do not belong. When it has not been done I have heard ordination sermons become stewardship sermons, and will never forget a Christmas sermon which prescinded entirely from joy or wonder at the incarnation and became an extended attack on the Supreme Court for its policy on nativity displays. In each case the preachers' real passion only appeared when these extraneous issues emerged and began to dominate both the time and impact of their sermons. Hearers of sermons such as these become confused and sometimes alienated.[22] This intrusion of foreign agendas is the peculiar trap into which those who do not write their sermons regularly fall, because these agendas will suggest themselves when the preacher is caught up in the experience of preaching or the excitement of outlining new thoughts. That is a time when the preacher cannot easily consider all the implications of what is being said or jotted down. Knowing what is on one's mind before preparing to write the sermon gives the preacher the freedom to treat or not to treat that material, in terms of what the texts and the occasion require. The results of this second step, taken with the rule that the Main Idea controls the content of the sermon, provide an important editorial tool for the revision process.

It is thus important to write down the answers to those questions, along with other personal reactions. Having them on a sheet of paper, or even in a journal, makes them available when revising the sermon and enables one to ask directly: "Have I been honest?" and: "Did I learn anything or grow at all in this process?" There is another reason to write these thoughts down. Writing them down, particularly when they are worrisome or distracting, is the only way many people have of clearing them from the mind so that they can work. On the other hand, some find this the way to discover what is important to them to deal with in the sermon. Thus this stage can provide questions to investigate when studying the scriptures. In some cases the sermon can begin to take form this early, especially when the preacher's main reaction is

---

[22] I am not suggesting that the sermon must stay where the people are, emotionally and psychologically. It remains vital to meet them where they are, however. See the "Pacing and Leading" section in the next chapter.

"aha"—the apparent discovery in the text of the answer to a vexing problem or important question.

Step Two is worthless without scrupulous honesty, particularly with regard to negative feelings. If reading the story of Ananias and Saphira in Acts 5 occasions fantasies about certain members of the parish, that fact ought not be suppressed at this point. It is very important data, as we will have reason to see below when considering anger and preaching. If the fantasy or feelings are not acknowledged, there is a greater chance of their appearing in the sermon in another guise and with negative results. If in revising the sermon, one has access to a list of acknowledged "baggage" brought to the sermon process, sermons are less likely to become the occasion for unconsciously settling old scores or creating new ones.

Students report that Steps One and Two together take between twenty and forty minutes, depending on how often they read through the lessons and how much thought they give to them, and that squares with my experience. Some report that they like to start Step Two, take a walk while thinking it over, and then come back to write their discoveries.

Step Three. We are still doing very preliminary work. Conscious of where we are in the liturgical year, and what significance the particular day has, read the lessons and psalm again, along with the collect, prayers of the people, preface, and if you like, the eucharistic prayer to be employed. Where possible, the preacher should consult the texts of hymns and choral pieces as well. The goal here is to look for common themes, or one dominant idea. This may for some people be the point at which the germ of the Main Idea is discovered; for most of us, it is simply a time of gathering possibilities.

The fact is that in the material there will be several, usually many, points of contact, threads, and themes, and the preacher will end up choosing one. Usually there will not be a general and all-inclusive theme which clearly dominates all the variable parts of the liturgy or even all three lessons and the psalm. Each liturgical component and lesson affects how the others are perceived. Given the fact, for example, that Episcopal Proper 19, like its partners in other lectionaries, has one collect but three sets of lessons, very different themes can suggest themselves as we go from the collect to the first lesson. The collect is "O God, because without you we are not able to please you, mercifully grant that your Holy Spirit may in all things direct and rule our hearts." In Year A that collect is followed immediately by: "Anger and wrath, these also are abominations, yet a sinner holds on to them. The vengeful will face the Lord's vengeance." (Ecclesiasticus 27:30). Year B, on the other hand, follows the collect with: "The Lord God has given me the tongue of a teacher, that I may know how to sustain the weary with a word." (Is. 50:4). In a day when many worshipers also have the texts printed in bulletin inserts, these differences in mood and content will be noticeable to many members of the assembly. The first lesson in Year A connects more closely to the first clause of the collect, and not unnaturally leads to consideration of the ways in which we are not able to please God. The lesson in Year B, on the other hand, might suggest looking for ways in which the Holy Spirit directs and rules our hearts. As we add other lessons and liturgical material, the variations increase. This is to say that there are many possibilities each week, and the preacher here is not to be a detective who sniffs out an immutable something which is "the" theme of the day. Rather, the preacher is surveying a huge treasure house from which one gem will be presented.

In the previous chapter I claimed that the lessons by themselves do not supply the theme of the day, but that any theme is constituted by the lessons, the other propers, and the place the day has in the church year. The general theme of the day's liturgy is only made specific as a given celebration and proclamation are planned. Another reason for this state of affairs is the structure of the lectionary. Often the first lesson and the gospel have common thematic material, while the second reading is a passage in a series from a New Testament book taken in course. It is unrealistic to expect that each sermon can do justice to all of the biblical material read in the service, let alone to all the other propers. The greats did not try most of the time: the patron saint of preachers, John Chrysostom, and his contemporary in the west, Augustine, tended to focus their attention fairly narrowly. It seems better to make what connections there can be naturally made to one theme or point. So in this step we simply begin looking for them.

This is the point at which I prefer to stop, as many do after the previous Step Two, take a break, and walk around the block or just sit and let all that I have read and observed coalesce.

Step Four. Choose the principal text for the sermon. Very possibly the observations made in previous steps will guide the choice made in this one, and the choice may be made for any number of reasons, some of which may be unconscious. *The text does not have to be the gospel.* I write this knowing that for many people the gospel is always the starting point of the sermon and for many of that group the gospel is always the text of the sermon. While they are free to preach that way, there is nothing in the rubrics or the literary remains of the great preachers to suggest that it must be so.

There are also reasons why one would deliberately choose texts other than the gospel. Our age is particularly aware of the story. Telling the story is how identity is formed and the lore and values of the group transmitted. There is no question that God's work in Jesus is the center of our story. Nonetheless, it seems insufficient or even dangerous not to tell the whole story. The history of Israel and the development of the early church, which are the subjects of the first lesson, together form the story of our ancestors. We can learn from and be guided and supported by their history. The moral and theological struggles of the early church, as attested to and addressed in the epistles, speak powerfully to our own concerns. In other words, freedom to preach on any of the lessons allows the whole of the scriptures to speak in the sermon.

Step Five is one of gathering data about the text. Preachers come with different exegetical skills, and it is well that we do not have an official exegesis of any passages. Nonetheless, there seems to be a minimum knowledge one needs to have about a text to insure that we have understood it and that it has encountered us on its own terms.

The first task is to get the best idea we can of what the text meant to the audience for which it was first written down, first made "scripture" in the root sense. Some preachers will also have the skills and interests to attempt to get behind the written text to reconstruct and analyze a passage's earlier history. As a minimum, though, we need to understand the passage as written. For me that means at least knowing of any textual problems, the social, theological, and literary context in which the passage rests, along with its authorship and date. This usually means recalling what one learned in introductory courses or consulting an introductory text or the notes of an annotated Bible. The chief goal is to understand the situation addressed and how the writer met it. If at all possible, after facility with sermon writing is coming along, this much should be done for each of the lessons.

At this point it makes sense to identify key words and concepts on which the author is relying. This is an important discipline, lest the text be treated too lightly. As a suggested minimum, isolate at least three words or concepts in the text for some study in depth. What does Paul mean by "righteousness" or "unbelief?" Think of the exciting study necessary to make sense of his dictum that "whatever does not proceed from faith is sin." What is captivating here is the opportunity to enter the world and mind of the writer, to understand the writer's language and intent. Far from being more seminary homework, Bible study in this sense becomes the chance for one person committed to the nurture of Christian souls to encounter the thought and method of the great ones who had the same task, to learn how they used their cultural and scriptural resources. Consequently this step is enriched by locating and comparing the text's scriptural parallels, in either form or theme. Locating verbal parallels is often as simple as looking at the notes in most Bibles or using a thematic concordance. Thematically similar passages, and those which take a contrasting point of view are not so readily located. Again, one's scriptural memory, formed by the daily office readings or other Bible study, is going to be the initial resource before the colleagues are consulted.

In addition, it is interesting to see what is being added in a particular passage to the reader's image of a character or group, especially in books which have undergone heavy editing. Stories in the saga of Abraham and Sarah often contrast strongly, and material from separate sources emphasizes different points in the lives of the ancestors. In another case, the bald statement that "The LORD would speak with Moses face to face, as one speaks to a friend" (Exodus 33:11) is followed immediately by an account in which a doubting and fearful Moses is denied just such contact, and pointedly so.

This is not an exhaustive catalog of exegetical tasks for preaching. It cannot be, as the levels and kinds of scriptural knowledge and exegetical technique which preachers bring to their task vary so widely. The point of it all, however, is to urge that preachers do whatever they can to hear what the text was saying, to meet its writers and first readers.

Before reaching for the commentaries or the capsule commentaries packaged with homily services, it makes sense for preachers to form their own opinions. With little more than knowledge of the Greek alphabet and the aid of an interlinear New Testament, for instance, one can have access to the wealth of information revealed by a Greek concordance or Kittel's *Theological Dictionary of the New Testament.* Even an analytical English concordance opens the door to real adventures of the mind. This is not at all to say that commentaries and capsule studies found in homily services should not be consulted. It is to insist that one never goes to a commentary except as one who has thought about a text and its problems or challenges, and formed some personal conclusions about them, however tentative. One then consults colleagues, senior colleagues as a rule, but colleagues nonetheless in the study of this passage. It also makes sense to consult more than one commentary to remain aware of the varieties of interpretation, and to make it clear that the preacher must make a decision about the text's meaning.

Upon completing this kind of study, as well as discovering the meaning and possible significance of other details of the text, including its geography, it is time to write again. Here we want a one- or two-sentence statement of the point of the written form of the passage to its original audience. Precision is important here: in order for listeners to know what the text is about it is important for us to be able to state its meaning clearly ourselves. We want to crystalize the meaning here, not restate the entire passage. Thus a statement of the point of the first lesson for Advent I in Year "A" might be, "Universal peace will result from all nations' submission to Yahweh's sovereignty, and God's people are to lead the way."

Ideally, in time, one will be able to do this for each of the three lessons, especially if the preacher saves journals and study notes. Certainly those who use any of the homily services or manuals on the lectionary will want to read the material on all three lessons.

Step Six. Here we leave the world in which the scriptures arose and consider the subsequent life of the text in the church. Isolate key theological issues raised by or implicit in the principal text. How have they surfaced or been addressed in the church's experience?

Here we encounter the cloud of witnesses again, as we consider, quite literally, everything else we know about the Christian tradition and the world in which it grows. "For here we have no lasting city" (Heb. 13:14), and the verses which follow, bring different things to mind when we consider the passage in the context of the theology of Augustine, Innocent III, Richard Hooker, and Harvey Cox. More theologically and socially loaded issues have a proportionately wider variety of application and interpretation. Again, there is no book that contains all of this material, and as one grows in knowledge of the tradition, there is more to draw upon here. The point of the exercise is first to remember that the passage had a life of meaning between its composition and our preaching on it, a life which to some degree still effects our hearers, and then to enter and explore that life as the text begins another stage of its existence as the church receives it this Sunday.

This is another point at which some people prefer to pause and let the material take shape in their minds. For me this much of the work is best done by noon on Monday, so that the harder interior work can take place as I go through the week.

Step Seven. This is the longest step. It is the one where we finally ask what the text might mean today. It is the step in which we ask how the words and concepts we have studied are applied to present day Christians.

There is a sense in which this step is the real work, for here preachers deliberately invite the word to search them personally. What does the text mean to you, with all you know about the Bible, history, philosophy, sociology and theology? What does the text ask of you? What does it give you? How does it fit into your own life of faith or cause that life to change?

This step starts with you, the preacher, before it takes up consideration of other hearers, and the reason for that is simple. If we jump here to what the text says to "them" without engaging it ourselves, we risk irrelevance, or worse, the doing of real damage, binding heavy burdens and not lifting one finger to help bear them. In addition, what is preached will never decline into idle speculation if it is part of the preacher's experience of faith or struggle for faith. Once again, we preach what we believe for ourselves.

Here one might consult the list of hopes and fears written down at the beginning of the study as we ask what this means for the preacher's own life. What does the text demand of you? What does it give or promise you? *How does the rest of the Christian gospel fit with or supplement its message?* That is, if the force of the text is to ask us some important question, where is the answer? If it places a demand, from where do the resources come to meet the demand?

The point of all this struggle is for the preacher to make personal sense of the passage or passages before applying them to anyone else. It is not to suggest that once you have worked it out for yourself, the job is done, and that once again this week the sermon will be about you. "As I sat down to prepare this sermon . . ." is possibly a productive sermon introduction once every six months at the most.

A good part of the work here is to sit and think. Leonard Bernstein once wrote that the best part of being a composer was being able to lie back on the couch and dream music, and when roused by critical family members also being able to point out that he was working, and that they should please respect that fact and not criticize or disturb him. On a less exalted plane, like his literary creator Arthur Conan Doyle, Sherlock Holmes would take in the data of the case, grab his bag of shag tobacco and excuse himself from Watson as he settled down to contemplate a "three-pipe problem." In either case, one is abstracted from other concerns and becomes physically passive, letting the mind work. I find it valuable to have paper nearby, either to record important thoughts, or to write down (and dispose of) nagging thoughts which interrupt with reminders of other business that needs attention.

For some reason many clergy feel compelled to look "busy." That is in part a result of their being compared (or comparing themselves) with professions and occupations which are driven by bottom line considerations; it is in part a reaction to the myth that they only work on Sundays; it is in part real guilt about the amount to time which is wasted. Nonetheless, the preacher does well to take the time to contemplate what has been studied, to ask some questions, and to enter as deeply as possible into the realm of the spirit, and to recognize this as part of the job, as being at work. It is well to have a place where this is begun. I had a very comfortable "sermon chair" in my rectory, in which I would begin to think about the sermon. Like most people, I soon linked a place and an activity, and things happened for me more quickly if I were in that place, or imagined myself to be. Your place may be the path on which you jog, or a quiet seat in the church. No matter where you are, it seems essential that protection from the telephone and other interruptions for half an hour be insured, so that the process may at least begin.

As already mentioned, I prefer to let this stage go on over two or three days, and find myself bearing the text with me as I go through other tasks and functions, giving thoughts time to mature and be questioned, occasionally making notes. There is no reason not to carry a tiny notepad everywhere to jot down ideas for further consideration.

Again, in this Step the preacher is asking three questions in particular. Some preachers will take them one at a time, others will seem to do them at once. I do not find that they are necessarily answered in order. Sometimes the process happens almost instantaneously. At other times I must use everything I have learned about meditation and contemplation.[23]

What does the text address in my life? With what new ideas, goals, demands, or challenges does the text present me? It may suggest that I think in a different way about people, events, myself, or history. It may suggest that I change behaviors or adopt new ones. It may suggest that I do less and think more, or vice versa. It may ask me to challenge the goals and behavior of institutions and groups to which I belong. What does it affirm about my present existence, and in what ways does it ask me to grow?

What obstacles, fears, sins, ignorances, limitations of mine does it point out? What burdens do I carry in regard to it? This gets a bit harder. If being "good" were simply a matter of deciding to be good, or if changing behavior were simply a matter of willpower, discipleship would be much easier. At this point we deliberately take the risk of having exposed to view our wrong or limiting beliefs, our misdirected energies, our egocentricity and laziness—and all the other things that are lumped under the word "sin." Whether one starts with St. Augustine's dictum that sin is essentially misdirected love, or else has a complex view of

---

[23] In addition to the more standard and well-known religious works on meditation, those who find it occasionally difficult to enter a creative state of mind might profit from John Grinder and Richard Bandler, *Trance Formations* (Moab, Utah: Real People Press, 1981).

society and personality as they effect behavior, the point here is to get at what it is in *me* that presents problems here, checking my own eyes for logs before examining the congregation's for motes. The task here is not to soften the demands of the scripture by explaining away inappropriate or wrong behavior, but to get at that behavior's root, so that change can occur. We risk this step in order more fully to appropriate the gospel, in order to be more completely transformed into those who know God and do God's will. If on the other hand, the text presents a problem which you have for the most part overcome, an area in which you are presently being blessed with growth, what was it like before things began to change for you? What incidents, sounds or images come to mind as you consider these things?

What has God done or what does God do about my concerns in regard to this situation? This is the hardest part of the task, and the one to which the most attention needs to be paid. To use a not altogether appropriate analogy, cure requires more skill than diagnosis. It just will not do to say: "I was wrong here, God forgives me, I will change," and let it go at that. We can do better than that, because God does better than that. These bones shall live.

For example, if you begin to discover that you do not risk social change which you believe is called for because of fears you have, there is at your disposal a tremendous Biblical tradition about God's presence with and vindication of risk-takers, and certainly our central story is about God's own Risk-Taker. How specifically has God seen people through times of change, in the Bible and in the life of the church? How does anything you uncovered in Steps Five and Six apply here? How do you know that your old ways are forgiven? What will happen if your choice for change means the possibility of getting hurt? Who will care? Who will help? What do the community, the sacraments, and the life of prayer have to contribute to you if you choose to step out of your fear? Are there things you can be or even ought to be doing to appropriate the resources you are offered? Are you alone in having this problem or needing these resources? What joys lie before you if you risk the change and begin to walk in newness of life?

When you have done this, there is a sense in which you have a sermon, Nevertheless, *it is vital not to stop here.* If you do, we will have a sermon which is largely about you each time you preach. Thus the question now becomes, in what ways is my experience with this text of use to the congregation who will hear this sermon?

In essence, one goes through the process of Step Seven again, with the hearers and their lives in the place where the preacher's was. Where is the congregation in its life? Given that, what are we all called to by this text, what thing or things stand in the way, what does God offer to make change and growth possible? What pains, largely invisible to others, must be taken into account and ministered to? How does God's love become tangible, useful, near and not far off, to those who will hear and be asked to change? How will they identify with Christ by taking on what you describe? What are their links to incarnation, crucifixion, and resurrection here? Have you ever seen such transformation take place? What did it look, sound, or feel like? How is it available to us all? What must they do to be saved in this regard? Making these connections means knowing the audience and their concerns. Thus it also suggests that there is a Christian duty to read a good newspaper.

The Main Idea

From all of this emerges the Main Idea, the end result the sermon is meant to have, the sermon in a nutshell. To express it, construct a single sentence, usually beginning "I want to get this congregation to. . . ."[24] A verb follows "to" and then comes the rest of the sentence. Almost always it needs to be a single verb. We are looking for something here which others might call the theme of the sermon.

Adequately refined statements of Main Idea are usually short and usually do not require qualification; they state exactly what result you seek. A clearly stated Main Idea might be, "I want to get this congregation to give more money," or "I want to get this congregation to integrate prayer into their daily lives," or "I want to get this congregation to share my awe at the incarnation."

Having a clearly defined goal for the sermon simplifies writing to a tremendous degree, and does a great deal to lessen writer's block. This Main Idea is the starting point for composition. When we plan the outline in the next chapter, the Main Idea is our starting point and goal. When we come to write the sermon, especially given the relatively short sermons our age expects, each part of the sermon is tested by whether it contributes to getting the Main Idea across. Stories, illustrations, and assertions which are really about something else are filtered by testing them against the Main Idea.

As I mention throughout, this is only one way to write sermons, and it produces a distinct kind of sermon. The outline of preparation that I have proposed has an implicit theology, and definitely engineers the preacher's values. It reflects my assumption that if you think your sermon must address a major problem you have only begun to preach when you tell people what is wrong with them. The model takes very seriously the

---

[24] As indicated in the introduction, I owe this formulation of the idea to the lectures of my own teacher, George Hoyer.

claim that "God did not send the Son into the world to condemn the world, but in order that the world might be saved through him" (John 3:17). It reflects my belief that God's fundamental attitude towards us at our most wrongheaded and destructive, is the desire that we experience repentance and new life, that we "might be saved" and that God's grace, justice, and peace be universally known and enjoyed by our resultant recommitment to discipleship. It reflects the Christian experience that coming to God redirects a person's experience, and that in answer to Augustine's prayer, what is commanded is also given.

Conclusion

In these steps we have met the scriptural text on its own terms, reviewed its history of interpretation, and finally asked where it intersects our present life. We have asked, for the preacher first, and then for all who will be hearing, what aspect of our life as individuals or community is addressed, often with change and growth in mind, and how the resources of our faith make such transformation possible. When we have identified an issue that is important for the listeners to address, and have identified as well the resources Christians have to meet the challenges the issue brings to them, we are ready to write a sermon.

6. Outline, Point, and Problem

ost preachers do not write out their sermons. Whether or not this is always a good thing is for discussion later. The observation is made here only as invitation to non-writers not to skip this chapter and the one that follows, as most of their emphasis is on organization and strategy. For that reason these pages may in fact be of special interest to those who decide not to prepare a manuscript.

The continued litany of this book has been that there are many ways to arrive at a sermon and that this is but one, one designed to get preachers started preaching and thinking about preaching. The refrain is repeated for the last time here as we explore a way of organizing and applying what was learned in exegesis and theological reflection. In fact, it is important to have more than one model in your repertoire, but the one presented here is a rather all-purpose model which it is hoped forms a basis for relevant and helpful preaching of the scriptures.[25]

At the end of that reflection process described in Chapter Five, we had a Main Idea, issues or problems it suggested, and resources appropriate to the challenges or problems we encountered. This work gives the preacher a basic sermon structure that happily falls into three parts, which George Hoyer called, Point, Problem, and Power for ease of recollection.

Those three P's provide a basic workable sermon outline. As I employ it, this outline has an implicit theology. First, it assumes that the Bible still addresses us meaningfully. It further assumes that this address will not let us go on in the old ways, and often calls us to radical change (repentance). But most of all, it assumes from the outset that there is and will be "power." That is, it assumes that in word and sacrament, prayer and community, contemplation and acts of discipleship, the Spirit gives God's people the resources they need to change, grow, persevere, and accomplish that to which they are called as they live new life in Christ.

It is important to note here that the anthropology of this model is quite high: we are called to great things by a Creator who values and trusts us immensely. The anthropology is also realistic about human sin and frailty as issues to be faced squarely that they might be healed or overcome. It does not suppose that all problems can be "fixed" and all wants supplied, but it does rest on the belief that even those whose call is to a cross will not be left without a Paraclete.

Thus the overall strategic aim of the sermon is to build up the body of Christ with mature members, not to infantilize them

---

[25] Several models of preparation and preaching are discussed sympathetically in Ernest Hunt, *Sermon Struggles: Four Methods of Sermon Preparation*, (New York: Seabury, 1982).

with guilt or with an immobilizing soteriology which lets each sermon be another call to get saved and lets it go at that. The sermon's strategic aim may be expressed as *transformation* of our selves, of our lives *and of our perceptions* of the people and world which we serve. Because that is the overall objective, the final P, the power, ought to get at least half the attention, at least half the air time, in a sermon. It is arguable that this final section should be planned first so that it gets the preacher's fullest energy.

Point. Problem. Power. You may wish to rename them as something you remember easily, or are more theologically comfortable with. My own second part, as I examine my sermons, tends to be more "issues" than "problem." In any event, there is value to this strategic structural approach: to have these categories in your mind is to have a notion of going somewhere as you prepare a sermon. To have them as normal mode of working is to be able, when necessary, to improvise like the great organists, who produce beautiful music while following carefully defined techniques and patterns which have become second nature and are only detectable to other musicians. They also provide a rather natural mental filing system for the many observations and reflections that occur each day.

So we prepare an outline. At the top of the page it helps to have written down the Main Idea, "I Want To Get This Congregation to. . . ." Very simply dividing the outline page into P, P, P for each of the sections makes organizing reflections easier. The outline is functioning not as edifice but as skeleton and organizer, an aid in attaining our strategic objective.[26] Here we organize and deploy the material we noted down during

---

[26] A word to computer users: writing sermons is greatly enhanced by learning to use the outlining program which is a part of most word processing programs these days. If yours does not have outlining ability, there are a number of stand alone programs available.

6. Outline, Point, and Problem   **103**

reflection, and add from our stock of ideas and examples. The outline is our plan for making the point, exploring the problems, and empowering action.

The Point

This is our "introduction." It has two goals: to establish rapport with the audience, and then to make it clear what this sermon is to be about and why it is important.

Establish Rapport. No one would begin a sermon by saying, "I don't want you to listen to this. I don't like you. I'm not interested in what is going on outside this pulpit today, and I am not happy to be here with you." In the same way, no one would start by saying, "I'm smarter or wittier or better educated or more sincere than you, and I want you to know it." We want to work as rapidly as we can to give the impression opposite to each of those negative messages, so that we can get on with the sermon, bringing the attention of as many people as possible with us. We want to bring speaker and audience together on the verbal and emotional levels so that this may happen. The better you and your audience know each other, the less rapport building has to be done in the sermon. When you are relatively new to the audience, the introduction can be drawn out a little to give hearers time to sort out your voice, mannerisms, and the rest of the non-verbal cues that make up a surprisingly large part of our communication. Assess the situation to determine how much rapport building there is to be done. It is particularly important when the emotional level of the congregation may be intense for one reason or another, to acknowledge it, to get with them, in order to move on. Just as the "power" section may be done first, *you may wish to do this part of preparation last,* in order to avoid distracting yourself in your job of setting out the Point clearly and invitingly.

The fact is that we do not have a choice about whether or not our behavior, verbal and non-verbal, influences people. It does. What we have a choice about is what kind of behavior we will display to hinder least and most enable proclamation.

Even in established relationships this "pacing," or building of rapport, is vital. Just taking note of where we are as a community, naming the condition, and moving on, can help. One device which establishes the wrong kind of rapport is a slightly aggressive, a bit over enunciated, and certainly strong "good morning," followed by an expectant pause for the response from the audience. This is how military commanders and headmasters once used to address their assembled subordinates, and has the effect of either immediately infantalizing the hearers, or irresistibly reminding those with more resilient egos of the first scenes of *H. M. S. Pinafore*. In any event, the way we say that in liturgical assemblies is "The Lord be with you."

Establishing rapport can normally be done with a sentence or two that connects you with the audience and moves to the meat of your introduction. It need not be structurally distinct from the part that gets to the point of the sermon: the right anecdote told well can do both beautifully. In churches where the sermon is begun with some kind of prayer, particularly Psalm 19:14 ("let the words of my mouth and the meditations of my heart"—often with the second "my" altered), rapport can occasionally be obtained that way, unless the prayer has become completely pro forma. Sometimes in established relationships, all that is necessary is non-verbal matching of the general attitude in the room: avoiding, for instance, coming on strong and loud to a perspiring August congregation struggling for air with cardboard fans provided by the local funeral home. In any event, it is important to *start* where they are.

Sometimes, however, rapport takes more than a sentence

or a smile. For example, Mother's Day is usually one of the later Sundays of Easter; sometimes it is even Pentecost itself. No one denies that each Sunday of Easter has an important message of its own in the liturgical year. That does not explain an odd occurrence, however. Despite the pews full of corsaged mothers attended by grown children who may not otherwise go to church very much and who have shown up precisely because it is Mother's Day, some preachers make it a matter of principle not to mention the holiday at all, much less preach about it, since the great Fifty Days are what they are there for. Worshippers by and large react by judging these preachers as eccentric at best and churlish at worst. In the main, interest and attention are not maintained in the congregation, except by those who keep wondering if the preacher will "bring in" motherhood in a kind of surprise ending. Whether or not Mother's Day should dominate or even influence the sermon content is a separate question, but supposing you have good reason to preach about something which has no natural connection to the secular observance, what can you do? Pacing and its consequence, leading, are your natural tools. None of it needs to be eloquent.

Pacing:

"Before we begin, [*making clear that somewhere else is our common and appropriate destination*]

it is a pleasure to note that this is Mother's Day, and I want to offer best wishes to each of you who celebrate with your loved ones today. [*important that it is you, wholeheartedly, not just a preacher bowing to convention*]

Later on, in our prayers, we will all

[brings it back from special group to the entire congregation and to the liturgical assembly's work of prayer]

have the opportunity to thank God for the women who gave us life, for the women who nurtured us, and to remember as well those of our mothers who have departed this life. I hope each of your celebrations today is filled with joy."

[the ambiguity is intentional here; some have had both a biological mother and others who played long-term nurturing roles, while others may have had people in one of the categories]

Leading:

"In fact, its a good day to be celebrating, because today as our great Resurrection celebration continues, we find our attention focussed on. . . ."

[Mother's Day is acknowledged and affirmed; its celebratory energy is going to help drive what follows]

The formula of recognizing the event, naming and respecting the emotions, giving them a place to go, and moving the audience together to a particular point or focus is particularly important at special events. Weddings, funerals, confirmations, Christmas, and Easter have in common the fact that many people who are not ordinarily in the congregation are there for many reasons, and in many emotional states. The beginning of the sermon meets them, welcomes them, and draws them to the content. The liturgy has other "gathering" moments, too. The most striking of these moments is probably an opening hymn with procession: there voices, breathing, posture and vision join to unite our attention and direct it to a single purpose and place. The other key gathering moment in some rites is the opening dialogue of the eucharistic prayer ("The Lord be with you. . . . Lift up your hearts. . . ."), which reassembles the community after the controlled chaos of the peace and offertory.

Making the point. This attempt at meeting the hearers where they are, of gathering them, is followed by (or simultaneous with) the introduction of the Main Idea. This can be done in any way that gets everyone to know what the sermon is about.

Our day has seen great interest in making the point by telling a story, either the Biblical story retold or else recast and explained or another story which leads to the same point. There are other options as well. Some preachers like to begin occasionally with ice breaker jokes, a practice which became quite common in Europe before the Reformation, but one not well attested in the first millennium. Others like to engage hearers by asking them a question. Another possibility in situations where great rapport already exists and time is short is to say something as direct as a version of "the lessons today led me to consider the intriguing point X, which is important because Y." However this introductory section is constructed, it should leave no one unsure of what the sermon is about: it is not cheating upon occasion to say at the end of the introduction: "Now the point of all this is . . . ," or: "So today's sermon is about. . . ."

A note about stories is in order, at whatever point they are used in the sermon. Their power is to be respected for several reasons. Listening to a story is an altered state of consciousness for the hearer, for whether the story is about the preacher's childhood memories or Ezekiel in the valley of dry bones, the listener ordinarily goes into a kind of "long ago and far away" mode. Because this is a mild trance state,[27] listeners are readily receptive to the many layers of meaning and suggestion in a story, receiving meaning on the symbolic level as well as the data-giving level. In a story there are characters, settings and actions, all of which communicate: there are no propositions to be debated, accepted or rejected. This is why sermons on the story of the Prodigal Son, for instance, are never as moving as the parable itself unless preached with or through contemporary stories. Perhaps it also explains why so few sermons are ever preached on the little-known but nearly overpowering stories in the Old Testament, such as that of Judah and Tamar (Gen. 38), but the sermons that are can be blockbusters.[28] Because stories, even made-up ones, get around the part of us that wants to argue about propositions, they are powerful ways to get onto the table ideas and possibilities that would not otherwise be entertained. Because they work on several levels at once, they have power to transform and even to heal.[29]

This being the case, stories should be used with respect for their power and potential. Thus, personal stories need to be, if not written out, gone through word by word in the preacher's mind before they are told in the pulpit. Otherwise a great deal

---

[27] The reader is asked not to react too strongly to this word: mass mesmerization is not our goal, and it seems that Svengali-type preachers do more harm than good. A trance is simply a state of highly focussed or unusual consciousness. Anyone who has just realized with a shock that he or she has been driving for twenty minutes without consciously paying attention to the road (while thinking about a sermon, perhaps) knows how easily and how often we slip into trances.

[28] This story appears in no Sunday lectionary, in common with several other stories of strong women.

[29] In this regard, see the brilliant example which forms the first chapter of John Kiley, *Self-Rescue* (New York: McGraw-Hill, 1977; repr., 1990).

6. *Outline, Point, and Problem*   109

of unplanned and perhaps unhelpful revelation can occur, with the effect of sidetracking the sermon, or undermining pastoral effectiveness, all without the preacher's awareness.

It would also seem that stories, whether Biblical narrative or a scene from a recent movie, must be told *as stories* and never told in a way that is appropriate to reading the news on the radio. Detail, voice, and "once-upon-a-time" quality count. Garrison Keillor's "Lake Wobegon" stories, most of which are thinly disguised sermons or morality playlets, certainly could be summarized in a paragraph of facts and precepts. However, they would lose their transforming power immediately, while retaining all their "truth." I listened once to the story of Ezekiel in the valley of dry bones being retold by a preacher who made us all feel its magic, made us know why and how the Israelites felt dead "and clean cut off." As he described their lost land, their lost children, their frustrated ambitions, and above all, their sense of god-forsakenness, everything in me that ever felt that way was there with them. And when he got to the rustle of the Spirit and the rattling of those bones as unexpected new life came to visit them and reconnect their broken and scattered selves, I was aware of how deeply I wanted a full experience of that life, and was ready, receptive, and paying close attention when it was about to be offered.

Less is more. Telling a lot of stories or using too many fantasy bits in a sermon has the hearer going back and forth to and from that altered state of listening to a story. Hearers report genuine fatigue from such a Ping-Pong experience. More helpful is the offering of just a few stories or images at key points and giving them depth and space to do their work, giving listeners time and space to enter into them.

Returning to the introduction per se, after rapport is built and the point made, no matter how, it is essential that it be shown that the point is important to the listener. "This is important because . . ." is a fine way to do that once in a while. Perhaps more natural, especially when a story has been told, is to connect the hearer to the story: "I suspect that most of us have had that happen and find it a challenge, and so I would like to look at it with you this morning." This "why it matters" part needs to be explicit. It is not safe as a rule to assume that the introduction has made its own point for everyone automatically. Not everyone has the intuitive faculty to see what is obvious to the preacher. Not all of us are masters of creative writing, and we need not be, as long as early on in the sermon we make it clear why the point matters.

A case in point. I once heard a sermon at a baptism in which the preacher began to establish rapport and make her point at the same time by talking about her childhood fears of monsters under her bed and the little theology she had constructed about them: as long as no part of her body was off the mattress, the monster could not get her. This theology worked while she was physically little and could easily keep all of herself on the mattress, but it was of no comfort as her body grew and she would awaken to find that she had an arm or leg hanging over the edge of the bed because she could not control her actions while asleep. As the preacher recounted this not uncommon experience the audience was with her, and many were visibly reliving their own similar childhood experiences, some nodding their heads in empathy. She made her point and showed its importance as she concluded her introduction by saying that there is a lot more in her world to be afraid of now, things that are real and come out even in the day time, and that little homemade rules based on the illusion of control cannot keep us safe, let alone happy or thriving. While she does not believe in the monsters anymore (almost does not, anyway), sometimes the terror comes back, but it is from things more real than imagined.

Now Stephen King would do one thing with the observation this preacher had made. He would tell a 600-page story for us which temporarily abolished the terror by using it in hyperbolized form to entertain, and that is fine. But in church we are not telling ghost stories around a camp fire. A sermon must do something else, it must face things as they are and apply the resources of the faith to them. The preacher in this case concluded the introduction by asking the question, how can we become equipped to understand and deal with the terror we feel in a world where we have so little real control? How we answer that question, she added, determines how we live. We knew that what she was saying mattered, mattered to the one baptized, mattered to us.

A similar point was made with entirely adult imagery. A colleague reports having his attention—and his most inner self-captivated by a preacher delivering a sermon to an assembled body of clergy. The preacher began by speaking of a eucharist he saw celebrated during an earthquake. The high point of the story was the dramatically described image of the priest elevating the chalice with one hand while pressing the other against the wall to hold himself up during the tremors. The preacher went on to say that his dual image of lifting up Christ and trying to stay upright oneself was one that often applied to the experience of ministry. My friend reported that this image, and how it was told, "made me give up things I wasn't ready to give up" and allowed those vital things to be dealt with in the sermon. Here the point and how it was told and connected to the hearers left no doubt about its importance.

Ultimately, of course, in any sermon "why it matters" is that God's will for us is to be done and God's gifts are to be accepted, if we and the rest of humanity are to be complete or at least fully functional. To the degree that God is again the center of our lives, to the degree that the Spirit is invoked, to the degree that love prevails and justice is done, to that degree will those elusive treasures called joy and fulfillment be found. Because the creation still groans waiting for that to happen, the sermon has its second section, which treats the problem.

"Problem"

The word appears in quotation marks because "problem" here can mean problem as in arithmetic, something to be challenged by and solved, at least as much as it means sin, deficiency or finitude. Challenges, issues, feelings, and understandings that surround the Point are examined and clarified here. What has to change if the Point is to be taken up and acted upon?

In Chapter Five we began to look for material for this section of the sermon by remembering that preaching (and life) would be very simple if we were entirely rational, conflict-free beings, rather like *Star Trek's* Mr. Spock. Sometimes that is the case, and people simply have the wrong information, and change when they get the right data, but that simple state of things seems to be rare in our lives. All the preacher would have to do then is state with proper authority how things ought to be, and we would perform accordingly. However, as a rule we find ourselves at best creatures more like Captain Kirk, basically trying to do a good job, but torn, with Spock's calm reason pulling us in one direction and Dr. McCoy's intense emotions and personal loyalties tugging in the other. When we add to the picture the dimension of sin, the problem intensifies, regardless of whether sin is defined as misdirected love, the self-preservation instinct gone wrong, or putting the self in God's place.

When the "problem" *is* sin, it needs to be addressed. How does one speak effectively of sin, sins, and guilt? How does one speak of sin and guilt in a way which gives people maximum safety, what therapists call "permission," to look at them, think about them? These questions are the subject of a book by themselves, but I offer here some general reflections on them.

Guilt first, because accurate descriptions of sin evoke the experience of guilt. It seems that the best thing to do with guilt, like any other emotional state, is to honor it, grateful for it because it has an important function. Guilt is moral pain. Like anger and physical pain, it tells us that something may be wrong, something that needs attention before the whole organism is destroyed. There is a New England saying that guilt is to be valued because it is as helpful as pain: without a functioning sense of pain you could lean up against a potbellied stove in a Vermont winter and burn yourself to death and not know it except for the smell.

Preaching thus does not avoid provoking appropriate guilt, or examining existing guilt for appropriateness. However, preachers must avoid manipulating by moral pain, just as they avoid manipulating by physical pain: the name for either kind of manipulation is torture. We name and face our guilts in order turn from them and overcome what lies at their roots.

From this it follows that the first thing regarding preaching about sin or sins is that sin is to be named, and named in a way that gives hearers permission to examine it, however tentatively. Mainline preaching has not always been good at this, often either avoiding talk of sin entirely or indulging in angry rhetoric. Essentially screaming at people that they are bad is not going to get many of them to examine themselves, and the evil situation addressed in the sermon will not be changed very much. On the other hand, failing to help people to examine their own sin is simply encouraging denial and spiritual atrophy.

Clearly some balance must be struck here. I am fascinated

by the psychological and sociological conditioning towards and "occasions" of my sins, but I also know that as a moral agent I must take responsibility for my actions. Blaming oppressive toilet training or a rough adolescence for my actions is not noticeably an advance over "the Devil made me do it," or "you'd act that way too if you had to put up with my life/job/loved ones." If we do not subscribe to the view that humanity is totally depraved, only able to will evil, to speak meaningfully about sin is to speak to people who are powerful, responsible, and able to take action. That assumption about them needs to shape how we address sin.

At the very same time, while it is essential that sin be named, it is crucial that the preacher does so in a way that its name can be heard and recognized. While some of us may not subscribe to a total depravity theory of sin, we do recognize that there is that in us which seeks our own will in a way frequently leading to distortion and destruction of the good. On the simplest level, then, it hardly makes sense for the preacher to appear shocked, surprised, or outraged to discover sin. Nonetheless, we seem plagued of late with sermons which are essentially angry denunciation, noisy preaching that is sometimes inappropriately termed "prophetic."

On "Prophecy"

There is perhaps no phenomenon which contains so much destructive feeling as moral indignation, which permits envy or hate to be acted out under the guise of virtue. (*Erich Fromm*)

My concern in the early part of this book was that Christianity's work and witness in the world need to be connected directly to its experience of God in Christ. God's people have always needed visionary leadership; they have always needed prophecy. Prophecy has a different starting point in the Christian experience, however. In Israel the prophets many times stood outside of the community they addressed, and often had no connection to the temple or priesthood. In the Christian experience, prophets exist within the community, and that relationship needs to influence their message, a message often delivered in the worshipping assembly. Truly prophetic preachers such as Martin Luther King, Jr., and William Sloane Coffin have directed, goaded, and even chastised God's people without ceasing to love them.

That is why it seems important to direct attention here to some of the preachers who style themselves "prophets," by which they usually mean that in their preaching they concentrate on diagnosing, exposing, and perhaps verbally punishing the ills of individuals, society, and the church. That this approach reflects an incomplete and very selective understanding of "prophecy" does not even require demonstration to anyone who has read all of Isaiah or much of Hosea, for example. After working intensely with students, and keeping track of my own inner state as I preach, I have come to believe that preachers whose main style is telling other people off (especially people who are not present) are to a significant extent hurt and angry individuals. If that is true, it is their problem, and one which they can choose to deal with or not insofar as it concerns their private life. To the extent that it creates unhelpful preaching it must be examined and dealt with, professionally if necessary. I address it here because I believe that when anger is unexamined it devolves into quite incomplete "prophecy" with two sad results. It leads to ultimately ineffective sermons and can mean personal burnout for the preacher. The question is not whether or not there is a lot wrong with the world; the question is how to be effective in changing it.

Consider ineffectiveness. The boldest statement one can make in this regard is that the Old Testament prophets did not get people to change very much, if at all, at least as the Bible tells it. The end of it all was that Israel was destroyed and Judah went into exile despite some powerful prophecy. That is the record, except for the preaching of one man who in all probability did not exist. Jonah preached judgment to Nineveh and the entire city repented. To him we will return.

If preachers have as their goal simply to be right regardless of their effectiveness, or if they have come to enjoy ventilating their angry and hostile feelings in a safe yet public place, they will not be swayed by my arguments. However to the extent that they really want changes to take place in church and society, the argument of inutility is important. The Biblical account is that prophecy was not the ultimate answer for getting the job done (Hebrews 1), so preachers need to be as wise as serpents and look for a better way to approach sin than mere denunciation. "Prophecy" as many of its present day exponents have come to characterize it does not work. The (incomplete, inaccurate, yet widely held) image of the "prophet" as one who delivers denunciation and demand from God is also an image of one who is largely ignored or rejected or both. That in itself may satisfy the personal needs of a few preachers, but our task here is to preach sermons which help people to make changes in their lives, so further inquiry into why the "prophetic" type of sermon yields such small fruit seems justified.

Suppose you hear a sermon, as I did, in the introduction to which the preacher likened the assemblies of the unrighteous celebrating their victory over Israel directly and without qualification to the victory celebrations held the night before by George Bush's supporters upon his election to the presidency. It was fascinating to watch people in the congregation, most of them liberal Democrats who were also quite distressed at the election results, tune the preacher out, permanently, at that point; they never heard what the sermon was really about because they were so alienated by the introduction. Although for the most part they shared the preacher's politics, they did not share the hostile judgments and rejecting attitude they heard, and reacted negatively to them. Some of them never made eye contact with the preacher again. The Christian assembly is not where we come to hear the motives of other people at once stereotyped, condemned, and dismissed. The preacher in this case ruled out any possibility that anyone who held differing social or political views might be acting with integrity or even general good will. Here is the listener's problem: is the preacher going to treat *me* the same way if I take actions or hold opinions which come from a different point of view? Can you imagine listeners seeking pastoral care or guidance from one they perceive as able to make such harsh and rigid judgments?

Some people report that hearing a good "hellfire and brimstone" sermon gives them what we would nowadays call an experience of catharsis. Having sat through all the anger and imputed guilt, and having taken their punishment by feeling bad, they feel that they have paid their dues—and have no impetus to change. That is ineffective preaching at its worst.

Others report that when the preacher "starts to 'should' all over me," the result is a sense of guilt and shame so overwhelming that a childish sense of helplessness takes over, and they do not feel as though a person as bad and stupid as they have experienced themselves to be in this sermon is able to do anything right at all. In the presence of this feeling of helplessness change does not happen. It is not even attempted, unless feebly as an effort to please Mommy or Daddy.

Still others react to perceived arrogance and insensitivity

in the "prophetic" preacher who always and only knows what is wrong with other people and society. No one wishes to seem arrogant, and we all react strongly when it is suggested about us. The chief way to avoid having the charge made about your sermons is to assume nothing about the inner state of people with whose behavior or opinions you disagree. J.M. Barrie once told his students at St. Andrew's, "never impute to an opponent motives worse than your own." Repeating Barrie's observation prompted a student to share the following account in a preaching class:

> Someone said to me about a mutual friend, "The trouble with him is that he hasn't suffered enough." I found myself withdrawing from [the speaker], because I knew something of how terribly [that person] did suffer in his soul and how much he had overcome in his past, and because, as I also see in retrospect, I wondered if my own sufferings were also being discounted.

Probably the greatest teacher of preaching in our century was Paul Scherer of Union Seminary in New York. Scherer was never shy about naming and dealing with sin. He nonetheless once addressed the present issue this way: "Be kind . . . be kind: everyone you meet is fighting a hard battle."[30]

After observing that "prophetic" preaching does not work as an overall strategy, it is important to identify it as part of a

---

[30] Paul Scherer, *For We Have This Treasure* (New York: Harper & Row, 1944), p. 55. Scherer's point brings to mind F. Foakes-Jackson's advice to a newly appointed fellow at Jesus College, Cambridge, words which preachers can also value: "It's no use trying to be *clever*—we are all clever here; just try to be kind—a little kind." This observation brings to mind the scene in the movie version of *Harvey*, where Jimmy Stewart says, "Years ago, my mother used to say to me, she said, 'In this world, Elwood'—she always used to call me Elwood—'In this world, Elwood, you must be O so smart, or O so pleasant.' Well, for years I was smart. I recommend pleasant. You may quote me."

burnout track. Because it cannot and does not work, this kind of preaching leads to frustration and to more anger at the community of the which the prophet is a part, and brings the preacher an ultimate sense of ineffectiveness and helplessness. It has pained me to watch and hear the steadily increasing frustration and uncomprehending exasperation in the sermons of "prophetic" types who reach positions of leadership in the church. They really do not seem to have insight into why their vision is not owned or supported by the faithful, and the pain it gives them can lead to ill health, professional disaster or "acting out" through personal misbehavior.

The worst part of all is that most people get their religious formation primarily in the hour or so they spend in church. Whether preachers like it or not, to a large extent they represent the church and even God to churchgoers. If week-in and week-out what congregations hear is ninety per cent condemnation, nagging and judgment, with a perfunctory touch of "gospel" at the end, is it unreasonable to suppose they will conclude that they are dealing with an essentially angry and rejecting God?

I once heard a preacher say that like his "prophetic" biblical heros, what he hoped would happen is that God would thoroughly humble the United States, bring some "really good defeat and suffering" to its people to straighten them out (and, he implied, also vindicate those who preached the truth). For those who hold his view we finally turn to the one prophet who did get spectacular results through preaching wrath, Jonah—who also had the advantage of being a fictional character. The story of Jonah is not, it seems, about the giant fish or even about the conversion of Nineveh. It is about Jonah and his attitude, a story intended to redirect the attitude of Israel towards the nations. In a sense it is the biblical antidote to Psalm 137, to risk an anachronism. After Nineveh repents we find Jonah outside of the city, and the kindest description of what he is doing is to say that he is sulking. The whining quality of his prayer is unmistakable.

"O LORD! Is not this what I said when I was still in my own country? That is why I fled to Tarshish in the beginning; for I knew that you are a gracious God and merciful, slow to anger, and abounding in steadfast love, and ready to relent from punishing. And now, O LORD, please take my life from me, for it is better for me to die than to live." And the LORD said, "Is it right for you to be angry?" Then Jonah went out of the city and sat down east of the city, and made a booth for himself there. He sat under it in the shade, waiting to see what would become of the city.

The LORD God appointed a bush, and made it come up over Jonah, to give shade over his head, to save him from his discomfort; so Jonah was very happy about the bush. But when dawn came up the next day, God appointed a worm that attacked the plant, so that it withered. When the sun rose, God prepared a sultry east wind, and the sun beat upon the head of Jonah so that he was faint and asked that he might die. He said, "It is better for me to die than to live."

But God said to Jonah, "Is it right for you to be angry about the bush?" And he said, "Yes, angry enough to die." Then the LORD said, "You are concerned about the bush, for which you did not labor, and which you did not grow; it came into being in a night, and perished in a night. And should not I be concerned about Nineveh, that great city, in which there are more than a hundred and twenty thousand persons who do not know their right hand from their left, and also many animals?"

"Is it right for me to be angry?" and "Should I not pity Nineveh?" are questions preachers need to ask before launching sermons which are primarily social or ecclesiastical critique. Jonah had to confront the fact that in his heart he did not want his listeners to change: he wanted to hold on to his wrath against them and see them subjected to divine judgment. This is why in Step Seven the preacher was asked to go through the whole process with regard to self before addressing the situation of others. Discovering God's care and guidance and help for ourselves as we struggle to become mature in Christ gives us the proper attitude towards God's people when facing hard questions and big repentances. Preachers have the great privilege of sharing with brothers and sisters what is true and helpful; this "brother and sister" ecclesiology leaves precious little room for scolding or belittling the congregation in the sermon. God appeals to the kernel of compassion still left in Jonah, if not for the adults then for the babies, and if not for the babies, then at least for the animals.

This is not to say that there is not a lot to criticize, a lot that needs changing. However, preachers will want to say more than "This is terrible evil. You are bad. God hates it. Don't do it." The fact is that people are not well motivated by negatives: the brain processes them strangely. Try telling a group of people of any age, "Do not think of a blue elephant." Most will immediately think of a blue elephant, and many will visualize one. We all know the results of "be careful not to spill your milk." The Commandments are no exception. "Do not commit adultery" requires one to imagine unfaithfulness to be understood. Worse yet, moral systems built on prohibitions produce the kind of legalistic piety which Jesus attacked in his generation, and which has never died out. It is the kind of religion which equates being good with not violating the code. It is the religion of Babbitts, the conforming legalists of the left or right. It is the kind of "loophole" piety which Arthur Hugh Clough could lampoon in his "The Latest Decalogue" almost two millennia after Jesus spoke. Among Clough's observations on Victorian society are the following:

Thou shalt not kill: but need'st not strive
Officiously to keep alive.

and:

Thou shalt not covet, but tradition
Approves all forms of competition.

Such a view of right and wrong keeps injustice institutionalized and always provides an excuse. Hence revolutionaries of the left and the right, once in power, almost invariably become tyrants or bureaucrats. For a while there is a new set of victims, but in the long run all that really changes is the faces on the money. The prophet Jeremiah knew that new hearts were needed, not just a shift in the power structure.

Following a pre-Reformation tradition, the Catechism of the Book of Common Prayer recasts each of the commandments in positive rather than prohibitive form. In this spirit, Jeremy Taylor had substituted the Beatitudes for the Decalogue in his liturgy during the Commonwealth period. The great exemplar, of course, is Jesus. Besides uttering the positive commands in the Beatitudes, he is recalled every Sunday in most Anglican churches as summarizing the negatives of the law with two *Shema*-like positive commands that we love God and neighbor, commands which require a total commitment of energy and will, commandments which have no loopholes (Luke 10:29-37).

This is not say that there should be no prohibitions—they are quite necessary on several levels—but it is to insist on the inadequacy of negative law in producing mature Christians, equipped for and performing every good work. "Divinization," as Eastern Orthodox Christians call spiritual maturity, is by no means the result of refraining from a list of prohibited activities. In the West, William Feather once said that at twenty-five we seek better laws in the search for a better world, and at forty-five we realize that what is required is better people.

To sum up, the self-image of our latter day prophetic types is based on a very selective reading of the scriptures. The real prophets taken as a group, looked for much more than a world where people stopped being bad. They sought a day when paradisal innocence would return (Isaiah) or a new heart be engrafted in humankind (Jeremiah), or when old and young, men and women, would all be visionaries (Joel). We started out looking for preaching which is "to the joy and edifying of Christ's holy people." Having people reduce Christianity to not behaving badly anymore, or merely altering their behavior by supporting the current (and ephemeral) ecclesiastical or secular agenda is to create a legalistic and smug little faith for those who share that agenda, and a defeating set of unreachable demands for the truly morally sensitive. It is also to write out of the church those who do not share the view of the moment.

How then, does one talk about sin, how does one effectively challenge people? The answer starts inside the preacher.

"Jesus, looking at him, loved him" before saying to him the most challenging words the rich young man was ever to hear (Mark 10:17-27). This concern and respect for the integrity of the hearer has to be the starting point, and is what made Martin Luther King, Jr. such an effective agent of real change where others just made noise: he understood that to work, nonviolence must be an emotional as well as a physical principle. You can "be angry and sin not" and still be effective, you can almost always be blunt and still be effective, but you cannot be rejecting or hostile and expect your sermons to work, for your inner state will contradict the tenets of your faith and violate the hearer as well. Truth, especially painful truth, needs to be spoken in love.

If you find yourself habitually devoting much energy to telling people off in your sermons, you may, just in the interest of effectiveness, want to put the brakes on. This might mean that telling people what is wrong with them or anyone else begins with a "Jonah check."

There are several elements to a Jonah check. First, do you feel angry? If so, do you do well to be angry? If so, name and deal with your anger in an appropriate fashion before constructing your sermon.[31] Second, do not prepare the sermon until you can visualize the individuals you are going to preach to, remembering their burdens, and thus looking at them, love them. Third, consider your overall strategy for getting people to adopt change—the sermon is for their benefit. If your anger was just, decide whether naming it in the sermon will advance or hinder the strategy. It is not always the case that naming it will help.

Scherer put it this way:

> When you look into the faces of your congregation, leave your disappointments at home, and turn your imagination loose in this amazing world. Speak to their other and better selves. They have burdens to carry and difficulties to overcome that they have never confided to you. If you know them as God knows them, or even as they know themselves: what they hope and fear; what they have allowed life to do to them; how they have been hemmed in and driven off in a corner; how lonely they are inside,— maybe you would feel toward them more as God feels. You might even stand in awe of them for all there is about them that is incalculably great.[32]

---

[31] See Albert Ellis, *How to Live With—And Without—Anger.* (New York: Crowell, 1977).

[32] Scherer, p. 47.

Another way to consider your attitude toward the hearer is to remember that Hebrews 1 and John 1 claim that when God really wanted to communicate, the Word became flesh, and thus Isaiah's intimations of Emmanuel, God with us, reached their highest fulfillment. The most important thing about the Incarnation is that it happened. As the Te Deum puts it, God did "not despise the Virgin's womb," choosing really to live where and how we live. In the same way, we started the sermon by establishing an external rapport, being with the hearers. That quality of being with them must reach its greatest intensity in what you say and how you say it when exploring the Problem with them. The much vaunted use of "we" in preaching can be effective here if used in ways that accurately express our shared humanity and its circumstances.

Thus "we" strive to help people to see beyond and underneath their behavior and attitudes to our common human afflictions and potentials. For example, telling people to give away their money to your cause (usually labelled "God") is easy; more challenging is understanding and bringing to light for the hearers those things in each of us which make this simultaneously the richest and least generous generation of Americans, then helping the hearers overcome them. Let's consider several ways to do that.

Preaching About Sin to the "Me Generation."

Many people of my generation and the first half of the one that follows have been called Yuppies, seemingly single-minded and unblushing devotees of the good life, to put it politely. To the extent that the characterization is true, it is a terrible thing. Now you can hate that about them and in them, or you can take them as they are, look at them and love them, and preach to who they are. Simply telling such people to tithe because the Old Testament once did has not produced good results overall. I have encountered several bad results. Some experience guilt. Many more have wondered aloud about a church which in so many areas has employed reason and tradition along with the Bible in addressing issues, often ending up with positions quite different from those taken in the scriptures when ancient writers addressed ancient situations. One person, an average lay member of my parish, said at a vestry meeting, "So when the Bible talks about money, we're fundamentalists?" How does one penetrate a cluster of selfish and defensive behaviors to get at what must be changed without resorting to biblicism?

One very direct strategy is suggested by the scriptures themselves. The much misused first chapters of the letter by the equally abused St. Paul to the Romans (not a uniformly unaffluent congregation, either) suggests an interesting model. Regardless of what we may think of Paul's view of sex, his view of sin in this passage is that *it does not work.* Idolatry leads to disaster. Those living in what historians were later to call one of the first great examples of an "age of anxiety" were being told here that the things they grasped when looking for a good and secure life just could not provide it; clinging to them brought negative consequences. Paul's bottom line here is rather like a Surgeon General's warning on cigarettes: sin is not good for you. It does not work; its effects are bad.

The preacher using this approach would want to demonstrate how hedonism and materialism do not work, do not provide security and happiness. This is best demonstrated through calmly described examples of cause and effect. Using cause and effect, linking their behavior to its results, is a way to describe St. Paul's revelation of the "wrath of God" in a way that practical people can hear without getting trapped in and immobilized by the punitive and hostile rhetoric common in the religious right. Fairly easy to describe are the physical and emotional traps of competition, stress-related illness, and waking up one morning to find out how ephemeral all these props are, because they are gone. Anyone who has ever suffered a significant robbery or fire knows how attached to things we are.

But that is only the surface of the problem, and reflection on the hearer's situation draws us to see the imprisonment of having things, how it is materialism which is the real opiate of the soul. We begin, when we think this way, to discover that we are talking about something more significant than attachment to things. Thus a second technique is both to intensify and focus people's awareness of their functioning values. Remember how the story of the rich young man ends. Jesus challenges him to give up possessions and status and follow him, to get his values really straight, and the young man goes away sad, not at all ready to let go of the things to which he clung. Jesus' own reaction is also sadness, and you hear the Word through whom all things were made expressing the creator's agony. Judaism, and Christianity at its best, are not world-rejecting, anti-material religions. Yet both claim that placing things ahead of spiritual priorities leads to big trouble, functional idolatry and moral anesthesia. Jesus expresses the bind with an almost audible sigh: "How hard for those who have wealth to enter the kingdom of God! It is easier for a camel to go through the eye of a needle than for someone who is rich to enter the kingdom of God." It is important that the preacher show the truth and effects of that teaching, to show how much we lose of ourselves when we feed our hunger for meaning and security with mere having. How difficult is it to enter God's reign?

It is especially difficult here in America, and now, and

growing more difficult daily. In conventional America of all classes and races, we are bombarded with a set of values which are those of having, with the result that we have confused the language of wealth and poverty, and do not hear ourselves described when Jesus talks about the rich. We do not say, "I'm not rich enough to have a second VCR." We say, "I'm too poor to have a second VCR." Even in a age of homelessness amidst plenty, children who have to share a bedroom (even though it may be larger than the apartment or hut which entire families occupy elsewhere) feel themselves deprived, feel "poor." Any insomniac can report that there really are people who watch the Home Shopping Club and phone in for revealing chats with the "hosts." There are game shows where the main event is a mad race through stores aisles with shopping carts: the contestant who grabs the most wins. The prize for soul-poison, at this writing, goes to "Lifestyles of the Rich and Famous," a television program which manages to combine the vices of exhibitionism on the one hand, with those of voyeurism and masochism on the other. The point is that in modern America, a lot of money is not needed to be a captive to the severely limiting value system of having things: it only takes a television set.

The hearer's situation is in part the fact that people are trapped and do not understand that their values and vocabulary keep them trapped. One trap is a sense of entitlement rather than gratitude, and thus the earth and its resources are to be plundered rather than received. Wanting, needing, and being entitled to something are no longer distinct categories. Can we keep in focus the truth that deprived of a sense of gratitude, an awareness of the gift quality of life and all that supports and enriches it, we are truly poor? In sermons it is important that we see that gift quality of life if Christians are to learn that possessions and responsibility are deeply related in the spiritual life. It is very hard to preach social justice to people who will only hear *"they* want more," and extrapolating from their own idea of what it means to want things, dismiss whatever appeal is being made. America's last frontier is pioneer individualism in its ugly vestigial form. Those of us not descended from America's indigenous peoples do well to remember that our determined ancestors, whether immigrants or freed slaves, certainly gritted their teeth and carved out a future for their children—but with a great deal of communal barn raising, midwifery, and shared labor. As a rule all we remember is the wanting, forgetting the interconnectedness that made the pioneer spirit functionally possible, and a potentially quite useful myth about our origins is reduced to one of aggressive individualism. The sin is in part our selfishness, in part our misdefined individualism, to be sure, and the totality of the sin is the larger endemic one that imprisons and alienates people.

If this description is accurate, how does one say so in a sermon in a way that gets people to look at themselves and acknowledge the problem on the way to healing it? On one level, one could just explain, and there are circumstances where this is appropriate: "I couldn't sleep last Tuesday night, and flipping the dial on my television, I came to the Home Shopping Club, and I saw something about our national life that made me stop and think. [Description] What that community of perhaps millions was gathered around was a definitely spiritual joy and fulfillment in having things."

Another way to present the problem requires less lecture material. One preacher did it with a story which on the surface took people away from the circumstances of our time and place and let their imaginations enter the question before their cerebral functions took over. The story is a long one, but here is a summary.

Long ago in India, at the time of the Buddha, there was a beggar woman who did not know it, but she was in fact the poorest beggar in India. This was because she was poor in things and also poor in her soul. She devoted herself to her begging, to thinking about what she would get and how she would get it so singlemindedly that she felt even poorer than she was. One day she heard that Buddha was invited to Anathapindika's palace in the Jeta Grove. Anathapindika was a wealthy householder and a great benefactor. So she decided to follow Buddha because she knew that he would give her food, certainly at least the leftovers.

It was true in India as it was in many lands of the ancient world, that the meals of the rich were a kind of public event, with spectators watching who was there, what they wore, and what delicacies they were served. After the ceremonial offering of the food, much like our table grace, the beggar woman, who had pushed to the front of the crowd, looked expectantly at Buddha. He asked her, "What do you want?" Surprised, she said, "I would like some food. I want the leftovers." Buddha paused and then, with eyes full of compassion, said, "Then, you must first say no."

"You must refuse it when I offer it to you." That is all he said, and he offered her the food. She found it almost impossible to say no.

In that moment, the hot Indian sun seemed even brighter as a new light flooded her awareness. For the first time, she felt shame. She realized that in all her life she had never said no. Whenever anyone had anything or offered her anything she had always said yes and taken it. She found it very difficult to say no, found she hardly knew the word. After great difficulty she did say no, and Buddha gave her, not leftovers, but the first courses from his own plate. And thus she realized where her deepest and most disabling poverty lay.

Such a story made analysis of the problem in the sermon easier. The preacher went on to observe that many people say they cannot support their church adequately because of the other obligations they have taken on, with no awareness of the fact that their values, their sense of entitlement to an artificially high standard of living, influenced the undertaking of those obligations. Certainly no one ever told them that following Jesus means deliberately choosing to live less well than your peers. The men and women who identified with the story of the Indian woman could realize that no one ever told them that they do not have to own the biggest house they can afford. They could become free to begin thinking about how they themselves choose to use their power, which is their money, time, and emotional energy.

There is much more to be said about preaching the Problem. Here I have asked the preacher before all to enter God's compassion for the Ninevites. Using the example of tightfistedness amongst the Yuppies of our day, several strategies have emerged. One is to show that sin doesn't work in the practical, ordinary world. Another is show how this practical inutility has a spiritual dimension which effects the whole experience of life as the issues of trust, identity and security emerge. A third was to explore values and to show their consequences for human society. A fourth was to allow the hearers to enter imaginatively into the experience of discovering the reality and the implication of the Problem. Having the advantage of knowing your specific audience, you will come up with better ones than the generalized examples found here.

The goal of a problem section is on the first level to identify behaviors and attitudes that need change. On a second level it is to intensify the desire for change and growth, often by effectively giving the hearer permission to acknowledge and explore areas of difficulty. Most of all, the situation as presented should have hearers intellectually and spiritually ready when you say: "Behold, I show you a better way."

7. The Power of God, Conclusions

f the point and problem sections of a sermon are effective, the hearer recognizes the need to change or grow, and also desires direction, intensified motivation, help, and encouragement in doing so. It is the purpose of the sermon's third P, "Power," to address that desire, to make clear how the point is attainable, "do-able." With such a definition, it is easy to see how this is the most demanding part of sermon preparation. The sermon will ask from many hearers a kind of death, a cross, as they give up or change familiar behaviors and attitudes. These hearers need the preacher's explicit care and support. Failure to provide it seems to be the target of Jesus' attack on those who bind heavy burdens and do not raise a finger to help bear them (Matt. 23:4).

The corollary of that observation is that the bigger the burden you bind in Point and Problem, the more effort you must make in the Power section of the sermon to be of help. This is true because in some sense people often need the sins that sermons ask them to give up. What we preachers often forget is that *all behavior has a purpose,* that there is a limited sense in which all intentions are good, aimed at sustaining and supporting the intender who may not or cannot see the intention's evil or mistaken side. If a parishioner on a skiing trip broke a leg and came into church on crutches, only a sadist would kick the crutches away, letting the person fall, on the basis that God did not intend for us to get around on sticks of wood. The very wrong or dangerous behaviors that you want to change in people not uncommonly serve as their crutches, not good healthy legs, but at least something on which they can get around in their environment. Very often on some level they recognize this, and may already feel pretty guilty and often quite helpless about it. Despite his affirmation of faith at the end of the passage, Paul's lament about his inability to match intentions and actions in Romans 7:14-24 is one with which many a Christian can identify. If the crutches must be done without because they are sinful, the preacher's task has just begun when that point is made.

If there are good healthy legs there, they must be identified; perhaps their use needs to be explained or modelled to those who have never tried them out. Very often people are simply not aware of the spiritual and personal resources they have been given or can appropriate. Having those resources and strengths identified can transform the way hearers identify themselves, and those who were once no people now find themselves with both identity and purpose (Exodus 19:3; I Peter 2:9f.). If the legs that are revealed when the crutches are removed are weak, or atrophied from lack of use, a plan needs to be laid for strengthening them while developing skill in using them, starting with the basics and building upon them, putting on the whole armour of God one piece at a time. Preaching the gospel to such persons often means starting them out on and supporting them in a journey of discovery, discipline, and development as their spiritual life deepens.

But what if there are no legs there? Then the person you are asking to drop the crutches is also being asked to accept a limitation in life, asked to do without an important illusion of wholeness. It seems to be the case that if substance abusers are to survive, they must accept a limitation: for some reason they do not process or relate to the substance in question the way that people they see as "normal" do, and must give up the illusion that they are normal in this regard, or at least must admit that they are different, not an admission our society encourages. Never underestimate the amount of genuine grief that is involved in such a decision, even though it be a lifesaving one. What is not always so clear is that renouncing some behaviors, as daily conversion to Christ asks people to do, creates voids which are not subject to a quick fix, and some have no fix at all. The grace that Paul found sufficient to enable him to live creatively with his unremovable thorn in the flesh needs to be detected and lovingly offered if new life is to follow the experience of death which we ask some hearers to undertake.

Thus preaching the gospel means pointing out strong legs, strengthening weak ones, and facilitating adjustment and compensation where there are no legs at all. More conventionally put, it means identifying the grace which conditions our existence and supports our life in general, and pointing to those acts by which God has entered history in the past and does so in the present. In the latter we make contact especially and above all with the work of Christ and the Spirit, church and sacraments, prayer and those acts by which we appropriate and develop God's gifts.

In Chapter Three I mentioned Paul's use of the expression "my gospel" (Romans 2:16, 16:25). Paul's use of the phrase was of enough significance for the pseudonymous author of 2 Timothy to adopt it as a mark of Pauline authorship (2:8), and is worth dwelling on in a chapter devoted to offering to people something of the power of God.

Paul had been preaching for at least a decade before he began to write anything that we have today. His writings, while often occasioned by something specific, thus also reflect the whole of what he has been thinking and preaching about. It is to this body of teaching that he appeals in Romans. There are competing views of the purpose of the epistle. The conventional interpretation of Romans is that it was something of a grant proposal. In this view Paul wrote it as a way to demonstrate his orthodoxy and thus his worthwhileness as an investment of mission funds for his projected work in Spain. More recently others have concluded that the book needs to be read as a treatise on the weak and the strong, another attempt to resolve the conflict between Jewish and Gentile approaches to what was beginning to emerge as Christianity. Paul's appeal is to his good news, his *euangelion,* a word probably to be understood in this instance as synonymous with normative proclamation of Christ *(kerygma).* His use of the phrase is his expression of willingness to both own and be held accountable for his distillation of the meaning of the event of God in Christ. He was willing to stake his credibility on that proclamation, proclamation from and by himself, but not—as he himself noted elsewhere—in essence about himself. The "Pauline gospel" emphasizes different aspects of relationship to the one Christ than does that of John or Matthew, for instance, and these writers serve to expand for us the vision of the good news that Paul presents.

These observations seem to lead to some general points about preaching. The preacher needs to know what and whom she or he believes, and be accountable for it. The preacher is also always on the lookout for new realizations and an expanded awareness of the limitless power of God, vulnerable to testing in that laboratory which preachers willingly make of their lives in this respect. Finally, the preacher needs to have the kind of self-knowledge that makes reflection and self-criticism possible.

Having made so bold a statement, I feel obliged to reveal "my gospel" as I can currently identify it, knowing before I set it down for you that it is far more myopic and incomplete than I would wish, and also knowing how much it has evolved. I am reporting fragments here, and have deliberately not tidied them up or filled in the obvious gaps: the reader will look in vain for a capsule theological system. What follows is a report of what has been on my mind and in my heart for the last few years.

The method. I include this material also to illustrate the method of finding out what one's gospel is. To discover what the core of my preaching is, I reviewed my sermons for the last three years, some in manuscript, some on tape. I tried to isolate in them not precise doctrinal statements, but descriptions of what life is like when one has to do with God.

I find many polarities, problem-power pairs, in my sermons. One pair typically begins with acknowledgement that, as M. Scott Peck wrote in *The Road Less Travelled,* healthy people acknowledge that life is difficult, sometimes even painful. Nonetheless, the difficulties and pain of life are what gives it adventure, purpose, accomplishment, and a good bit of joy; difficulties are also places where one can meet God and oneself in new ways. They are often places where we discover that the God who did not abandon Jesus in death gives new and greater life to those who face life's issues head-on. As the first chapter of this work reports, I find great encouragement in the notion of Jesus as pioneer, beckoning us to follow, stripped of all impediments, running the race, the crowd of saints cheering us on.

That active pair, difficulty and resurrection, is itself in tension with another more interior pair, lostness and adoration. Doing, creating, and meeting challenges are all fine things in their way, but unrelieved they isolate us from communion with "life, the universe, and everything," which simply become that which conquers or is to be conquered, and the more one achieves, the more isolated and rootless one can become. It seems that we are built for more than subduing—or dominating by understanding—our environment. We are saved in part by returning to communion with it, and with God at its base. Thus I increasingly sense an imperative to garden, to rejoin and tend life. More especially as I have come to know scientists among my students and parishioners I have been helped by them to an expanded awareness of the vastness and workings of the universe and its internal relatedness. In so doing I have begun to sense a quiet ability to be again a creature, part of it all, an experience quite alien to most of my religious formation and certainly alien to our work-ethic society. People living in urban areas seldom even see the stars anymore, and we find it a positive treat when the stars are out, but life and the universe can be contemplated everywhere. It is in moments of this contemplation that I find that I identify most deeply with Psalm 104 and with the central character in one of the first "beatnik" novels of the 1950s. The spiritual odyssey described in *The Dharma Bums*, concludes with words that have never lost their power to move me:

> Now comes the sadness of coming back to cities and I've grown two months older and there's all that humanity of bars and burlesque shows and gritty love, all upside-down

in the void God bless them. . . . Down on the lake rosy reflections of celestial vapor appeared and I said "God, I love you" and looked up to the sky and really meant it. "I have fallen in love with you, God. Take care of us all, one way or the other."[33]

The importance for my preaching of this awareness of our spiritual foundation in the life of the cosmos is that it provides transformation of personal experience and of perception of others, and I can find myself learning to reverence the life that is in other people more than trying to correct them. I have only begun to learn the necessity of physical well-being and exercise to experience the world in this way, but find myself in middle years revelling in myself as creature in a profoundly spiritual way which does not exclude physical exhilaration. At its core is the realization that life is a gift, not a task, and that the gift brings with it an invitation to participation in the giver.

At the heart of both the active and the receptive relationship to life is the experience of God as "being there," supportive of and present to us. This is how I have come to speak of the Incarnation. There is no part of our life that God does not know, that Christ has not taken into the Godhead. Calling upon God means calling upon one who knows joy and suffering, death and life. Calling upon God means calling upon one who came among us in complete and unrelenting love.

Only slowly have I been able to cross the years and the cultures imaginatively and really come to believe the commonplace that Jesus shows us what our life is meant to be like. The key seems to be in the depiction of Jesus "knowing he had come from God and was going to God" (John 13:3), laying aside his garments and acting as a slave as he washed the disciples' feet.

---

[33] Jack Kerouac, *The Dharma Bums* (New York: Viking, 1958), p. 244.

Real life, extraordinary life, is lived in conscious relationship to God, who is its source and destiny. When we know that about ourselves, we live differently, for our acts have higher significance. Viewed this way, Jesus' actions do not appear quite as random as a first reading of the gospels suggests. Table fellowship with notorious sinners, linking forgiveness or faith or both to healing, keeping a wedding party going, deflating religious ideologues, feeding the multitudes, calming the storm, withdrawing to rest and pray, and so on, all add up to one who comes that we may have power, what he calls life in abundance. Here was one truly come not to condemn the world, but come that the world might be saved through him.

How then does one get saved? How is it true that "In Christ God was reconciling the world to himself" (2 Cor. 5:19)? Clearly those who followed or accompanied Jesus received new understanding of themselves and the world. The transformation of Zaccheus' life and the witness of the Samaritan woman at the well attest to that. But the cosmic drama of God's transformation of the world was to focus on the manner as much as the fact of Jesus death. Who dies and how he dies are both important.

I have described the one who dies as him who was consistently, wisely, unsentimentally, and fully present in love. Sin and evil are revealed for what they are in attacking such a person. This is precisely why it will not do to argue about whether the Jews or the Romans bear the blame of killing Jesus. When I read the accounts of Jesus' passion, I know who kills him, and here my verb is in the present emphatic.

Despite living almost half my life in an intensely cross-focussed ethos, my heart is left strangely chilled by conventional Catholic and Protestant recourse at this point in telling the story in forensic language of Jesus bearing the burden of our sins in such the way that he pays a price or satisfies a judicial demand, as biblical as such metaphors may appear to be. In such systems God is always made out to be rather an ogre or at best a split personality. The cosmic dimensions of the passion narrative move me to something quite beyond double-entry book keeping.[34] We see in it again something of the image presented by Hosea, the Almighty become a grief-torn lover, wooing back an estranged and unfaithful spouse. Jesus' sacrifice takes on dual significance. The complete human being ("Son of Man"), he offers his will and life to God's purposes without reservation. At the same time he offers himself to us, at our hands.

I say this because when I look on the one who was pierced, I do not see Caiaphas or Herod or Pilate, or even Judas or Peter as themselves. Who does not know what it is to preserve a family, a job, program or institution at the sacrifice of an individual or two? It is not even necessary to assume that all of the religious leaders who condemned Jesus had anything personal against him: they were quite arguably doing their job and some may have even felt a moment's regret at the loss of a young man of promise. Pilate's careerism requires little comment: who does not wish to appear to be "Caesar's friend" at work, in the community, even in religious assemblies? And we have so many Caesars. The dilettante Herod rather likes religion, but does not really want to get any on him. Judas' betrayal and Peter's denial of Jesus confront us with the times when our beliefs or our need to survive displace personal loyalties and relationships in ways too painful to recount coldly here. The noisy and fickle crowds still live in every lynch mob of the left or right, in every jerking knee, on every occasion when the herd instinct of "decent people" displaces reason or compassion or both.

---

[34] That the double-entry accounting system was invented by a priest is a fact of cultural history worth considerable contemplation.

Although these biblical characters, except for the crowd, are all certainly men, all probably Caucasian, all Jews or worshippers of wood and stone, all living so very long ago and speaking other languages, the limits of sex, race, religion, culture and time are crossed when this story is told. I not only see myself, and you, gentle reader, killing Jesus then and now, I see him who is love very unmetaphorically bearing the sins of the world. It makes all the sense in world for the soldier at the foot of the cross to figure it out at the end: this is God present for and with us. At our very worst moment the legions of angels do not appear like the cavalry to save and avenge, and in fact Jesus rather generously prays for us as though we do not know what we are doing when we kill him and so many others, often dispassionately, often automatically, often for what we think is a good cause.

Recognition of or revulsion at the evil which is business as usual in the world is indeed redemptive when it changes behavior, drawing us to the divine mission of love which even the agony of the cross could not force Jesus to abandon. However, except for the few people given to morality, neither the story of the death of Socrates nor that of Jesus effects much personal change. In fact, the story this far runs the risk of dissolving into catharsis, a tragic piece about the cussedness of things, to be played along with *Oedipus Rex* or *Romeo and Juliet*. There is the odd fact that our hero here has no flaw except that it occurs to us in our worse moments that he possibly carried love and sense of purpose just a little too far for his own good. Nonetheless, in viewing or hearing these tragic stories we get to snuffle a bit about the world but in the end fold our programs and go right back to it. Bad as it is, that world is the only reality we have.

Or so we think. But a new reality is offered, one which transforms me, saves me. What startles and attracts me, in fact compels me, about the resurrection accounts is the way Jesus appears. His tenderness to Mary in the garden is comforting and makes good sense; what is stunning is his interaction with the disciples. With one exception they had betrayed, denied, or deserted him in his most trying hour. Yet his repeated greeting to them is "Peace be with you." It is here that I think I have learned what "forgiveness" really is, how thoroughly radical an expression it is. Jesus had quite literally borne the sins of these people, had experienced the pain of their actions, had in fact died; on the other side of that experience, instead of reproach or I-told-you-so, he offers a restored and continued relationship, one in which he has now invested his pain. In one story Peter is even given the chance to rehabilitate himself: "Peter, do you love me?" In confronting the one who bore the sins of the world, who bore my sins, returning to offer peace, I am shaken to my roots, and know the cosmos in a new way.

It is from this utter consistency and triumph of divine love that I conclude that there is another reality, one that starts with my responding to those words, peace be with you, with Thomas' "my Lord and my God." For our sake Jesus has taken on the pain of the deserted father in the prodigal son story: when we return there is only the embrace and the feast. That is one side of the new reality, a side which turns my expectations upside down, dispels guilt and fear, and lets me experience the peace of God.

The reality of the cross and resurrection is even greater than my rather private and individual experience. The reality offered here is the reality that we only really live when we do as Jesus did, loving consistently, fully, and actively. It means that the only way to deal with the world is to face it for what it is and to love it. This way of loving the world also means caring enough to confront and name its evil. It means that the only path to overcoming estrangement and sin on the personal level is to die on the cross: letting ourselves actually feel the hurts we are tempted to deny or resent or be enraged about, and surviving that pain find ourselves able to love freely, and find ourselves growing in union with God.

To come to the eucharist, no matter how one answers the questions of presence and sacrifice, is to encounter a deep paradox: the signs of death, broken body and poured out blood, are also the signs of life. Similarly, the drowning of baptism is also cleansing and rebirth. These rites are about how one appropriates and lives the new reality.

In telling the story I confront my sin, but find God's love overcoming it, restoring me, and calling me to a new way of life, one which offers each of us quite attainable fulfillment and even a measure of greatness. The address to Peter now comes to me. "Do you love me?. . . . Feed my sheep." Life thus redefined is both less stressful and more demanding than making it to the top of the heap in the old reality.

In trying to live any of this out I have come to experience the power of supportive community both on the level of the encouragement that being in a crowd of like-minded and similarly intending people gives, and also in the small-group and one-to-one struggles to understand, focus, or just keep going. I have discovered that there really is only one way to find out if any of this is true, and that is to try to live it, to try to love and to try to practice the presence of God.

From this trying to do it, what some might call discipleship, I have concluded several things which recur in "my gospel." There may be some in our world who need to hear, "Anyone unwilling to work should not eat" (2 Thess. 3:10). There may in fact be others who need to hear that unwritten Protestant scripture, "God helps those who help themselves," and who need to actualize themselves. Like many productive, prudent, essentially hard-working types who make up the bulk of the sermon audience and who want to follow Jesus, I need to hear something else. The first conclusion I have drawn from trying to live that discipleship is the dual apprehension that God did not bring us out into the wilderness to perish, *and* that we have here no lasting city (Exodus 14:11 inverted; Heb. 13:14). I find myself both led and sustained in often unexpected ways, yet it is also true that there is nothing to hold on to that cannot vanish in a minute, and that when I grasp for permanence I usually defeat myself. For myself, given a marked tendency to over-plan and to manipulate for the illusion of security, "give us this day our daily bread," offers both a correction in where my energy is directed and release from anxiety. I have no idea how long or how comfortable my physical existence will be, but I have a growing core of belief, tenuous enough to be far from complacency, that I am free to go where I am led, because "whether we live or whether we die, we are the Lord's."

"Where I am led" implies my experience that God is accessible, and that prayer involves first of all opening oneself to God. The qualities of surrender and listening for God are essential to prayer. We live in an age when one risks being locked up as psychotic for claiming that God communicates, and yet in one way or another that is what happens—at least when we learn to listen. Deep within us the Spirit really does breathe, and we are invited to enter those depths in surrender to and in encounter with God. In this relationship to God we discover the unnerving truth that God acts. God heals us, gives us more than we can ask or imagine, and enables us to become agents of change in an unjust, painful and starving world. Such transformation can be frightening business, and thus the supportive and reinforcing functions of church and sacraments grow in importance as one enters more fully into life.

In sum, for me all of this means purpose and power in living. Life, although at times challenging, is a gift to be used, enjoyed, and managed in consultation with the giver. Again, life is not a task, not a jungle through which we must hack our way blindly, hoping to reach civilization. Each present moment with all its potential is a gift. The great and burning question of stewardship in our church is not really about what one pays back. First of all it is about the acceptance of life, of the succession of present moments with their power and resources, as a gift, something from outside ourselves, something to be enjoyed and managed appropriately. Stewardship is then a question of meaning: what do I want this life to stand for? Finally, "what" is addressed in "how"—what commitments do I make to realize that meaning if I am to take myself seriously about it? Receiving and enjoying the great gift of life means both discipline in applying what is known and openness to receiving the new. Discipline means as well taking discipleship seriously and practicing it methodically: neither spiritual formation nor social action is optional for those who make anamnesis of the incarnate Christ.

Those are the main points of what I have found myself to be saying over the last few years. Upon rereading them I find how much they inevitably reveal about my personal agenda of late, and what they suggest I need to shore up. But doing this kind of exercise also reveals to preachers that their faith has increasing depth, that they have something they believe to be worth sharing.

Implications for Preaching

I recently said to a colleague that I was going to include in a sermon a reflection on Woody Allen's line, written in his thirties, "My one regret in life is that I am not somebody else." My colleague, in his late sixties, replied without any pause, "At my age, I'm amazed to think of all the different people I have been."

Samuel Proctor once reminded students at a General Seminary colloquium that he found himself having a quite different agenda in preaching every few years, and had come to accept that as he developed and changed as a person, new experience and new insights would cause great shifts in the content of his preaching. Even St. Paul, who can contend in Galatians "not that there is any other gospel," has different emphases and a different agenda in others of the writings generally thought to be his.

One can rely on the lectionary and the liturgy, as I hope the opening chapters have made clear, to balance this reality to some extent, but if you are aware of what emphases are currently captivating to you, what life-business is currently being done in your experience, those personal interests can be kept in balance, and also explored and worked through in creative depth.

Just as the preacher's life is in process, so is that of each of the listeners. The "power" part of the sermon needs to respect that about both preacher and listener. Not everyone in the audience is in a place where they can hear (or bear to hear) your point and problem in any depth. Of those who can and do hear, there are people who are facing life in widely different ways, so it seems that preaching Power must deliberately cultivate variety. Those who cannot hear and act today are quite likely still listening, storing impressions and images for when the time is right for them to act.

The power section of the sermon explores how life with God assists us in growth and transformation. It makes connections and offers direction and resources. Linking my story with that of God's people of the past changes my perception of it as isolated agony. Teaching me how my perception of God becomes practical moral vision gives me purpose. Inviting me to pray and suggesting how to do it helps me find the solid core within me from which authentic action is possible. Pointing to the resources of church and sacraments ministers to my fears and sense of weakness.

More specifically, this appears to be a time for the church to reinforce the christological aspects of its preaching. This is so because much contemporary preaching has not made sufficient connection between the preacher's desired outcome and its foundation in the gospel, leaving the audience to think that they are hearing a new and perhaps not orthodox theology. By making the connection, the preacher can show them that newness and orthodoxy are not mutually exclusive. Why is Jesus important in your sermon? In the model I have set out above, I find that Jesus is the true human being who not only shows me what life is, but is also he in whose life, death, and resurrection my existence is changed. In relationship to him, to his history, we receive power to live well, and to learn what that expression really means. Thus it is important that our preaching not trivialize Christ: to do so is to distort the foundational relationship the hearer has to God and self. "Looking to Jesus" means seeing more than an occasional good example or painting an essentially emotional picture of "the Redeemer." Dorothy Sayers put the problem this way: "Not Herod, not Caiaphas, not Pilate, not Judas ever contrived to fashion upon Jesus Christ the reproach of insipidity: that final indignity was left for pious hands to inflict."

This is said not because I have an ideological need to tighten up our commitment to Chalcedonian doctrine. I am rather concerned that we often seem to miss what can give Christian preaching cohesion, authenticity, and functional usefulness. The preacher does well to connect "my story," "my problem" in some sermons, with Christ. How did Jesus address this issue? How does his function as "pioneer" help us to meet it? How does he love and help me when I am caught in this predicament, even this sin? How is his continued presence with the Church of use in this situation? How does remembering him embolden, encourage or direct us? How do the gifts of the Holy Spirit make this real for us?

The more I become convinced that we are made for a vision of and union with God, and that Christians are being transformed in that direction, the more important it becomes for sermons to reach for the depths of what we have so inadequately come to call "the Christ event." There we find ourselves known, put into context, directed, and supported as we move toward God, not away from, but in the center of the world.

So far several points about the sermon's third section have emerged. We connect the problem to the resources of the faith by answering questions such as how is God with us in this, what helps, how does Christ enter this picture? How do we help people experience the fact that the Son came not to condemn them but to give them salvation and power? How, in short, does my story connect to the great story?

Nuts and Bolts

There are some specific techniques worth considering in writing about power. The first may seem obvious, but experience suggests that it is not obvious to everyone all of the time. *Be sure your sermon addresses the issues it raises.* Beginning preachers especially will raise as point or problem some important or highly charged emotional issues and thoroughly get the congregation's attention, but not ever address those issues in the third and most important part of the sermon, even in passing. The questions you raise should be answered, even if the answer is that this is an issue with which we must continue to wrestle, and here is what we can do in the meantime. Preachers who like to begin sermons with a question have a natural conclusion handed to them on a platter if they end by reminding people of the question and how it has been answered. If the goal of the sermon has been to get people to start thinking about something, some question which you may wish to remain open, you still have spent time in the sermon explaining why the question is important and what they have at their disposable in starting to engage it, and the same kind of connection can be made. Simply put, then, if you start by raising the issue of child abuse, do not respond by giving advice about crop rotation. Most of us get good or exciting ideas while writing, and may be led into paths far from our initial question, so this point is where a functional outline helps us stay on track or to lay completely new track. One way or another the train announced for Harrisburg should not arrive in Hartford. Other valuable insights that occur along the way can and should be saved for another occasion.

Because people are different in their history and perceptions, it is valuable to include in sermons more than one kind of resource, more than one kind of power. One might prepare a little mental check list. What knowledge do people need? How can those who learn by experience get the message? What are the links between our story and the one that the text presents? What is offered for contemplative types to ponder? What in our experience of church and sacraments helps? Where is the Spirit to be encountered?

Another way to approach this question is to develop some knowledge and skill in accessing perceptual systems. Most people organize their world and file information visually. The next largest group do so kinesthetically, with reference to internal feelings or external spatial relationships. How they felt about what they learned or where they where in relation to an event or speaker is usually their key to recalling information. The smallest group of these three (and there are others) do so with reference to the world of sound and speech. The key for preachers is to remember to address all three channels, and to move between them. For some reason, it is in the slight disorientations in switching frames of reference that change can take place at a rapid pace.[35]

On the more manipulative side, this is how powerful sales personnel close deals. They are taught to say to people whom they perceive to be visual: "Look at the . . ." listing all the visually impressive features of the car, concluding: "Can you see yourself in that?" When they detect that you are visualizing, they quickly make the switch, to "Doesn't that feel great?" And it is only a few seconds in that shifted and mildly disoriented state to "Would you prefer morning or afternoon delivery?"[36]

It is precisely this manipulation that we wish to avoid, while appropriating the resource which is being distorted in the sales technique. Remembering the rule that in any communication, you cannot not influence, the question becomes how to influence in a way that respects and does not manipulate the listener. When preachers make abrupt shifts in sensory reference system, they do so to offer a new possibility which the hearer is free to accept or decline. This is another way to employ the pacing and leading techniques given in the sample Mother's Day/Easter introduction above.

A student preached an essentially well done Good Friday sermon to our class, one which ended with a striking description of the face of the crucified Jesus lying in repose. Nonetheless, the sermon had a flat or somewhat maudlin effect on us: the

---

[35] A book helpful in understanding this and many other aspects of communication is Genie A. Laborde, *Influencing With Integrity* (Palo Alto: Syntony Publishing, 1983).

[36] The reader need not take my word for this. Laborde outlines successful sales techniques used by sales people who have become millionaires. You might also recall unwanted and unneeded purchases you made recently for reasons which still appear to be mysteries.

preacher had not really expressed what he was getting at and perhaps did not know yet himself. It seemed to some extent that we were looking at Jesus but did not know why. In our discussion group I asked him to add another paragraph: "You've described the face of Jesus so movingly, X, that I wonder what that face wants to say to us." That shift jogged his creativity as preacher and ours as hearers as he immediately extemporized a powerful and effective closing section for his sermon.

Thus a student preaching on Jesus' discourse to the disciples on the road to Emmaus and focussed entirely on what Jesus was saying, gained new power for his preaching by shifting to the visual and kinesthetic content of the Lord making himself known to them in the breaking of the bread, their hearts burning within them.

Inviting people to "imagine" (never "pretend") themselves in the story, or to imagine themselves trying on new activities and experiences is the beginning of making those new things reality. This is particularly true if the imaginings are tied down to what they might see, feel, do, or hear.

This is best done indirectly. Beginning with "Now we are going to meditate and imagine" is pretty sure to evoke resistance. A preacher who maintains good rapport in a sermon can describe an event and move to "And I wondered what it would be like for you to see yourself in that story," making it easy and natural for the most practical of people to experience visions and new realities.

With a vision or new understanding in place, the 76% of the population who are sensates still want to know how to achieve it. There are degrees to which the largely intuitive preachers should and should not give in to this implicit demand. Each sermon probably should share some of the how of spiritual growth, point to some of the resources in place: I have usually tried to attach to sermons things hearers might do or think at carefully selected points in common experience that coming week. "When you look at yourself in the mirror tonight, say..." or: "When you sit down to dinner, you might remember that..." or: "When you read the newspaper tomorrow, look for...." Such invitations have the effect of anchoring what you hope will happen to something you almost certainly know will happen. Particularly when helping people deal with deep-set problems or sins, alliance must be struck with just as deep-set behaviors that are neutral or positive.

For a mundane example, one Advent it seemed important to me to address the frenzied madness that overtakes most people at Christmas time, leaving them too exhausted for meaningful encounter with the incarnation. I was already on record as opposing Scrooge-like sermons by clergy who preach against the secular observances that attend Christmas, so my tactics were limited. Rather than raging against all the things that distract us from Christ at this time of year, I tried to reconnect them to what the holiday is about. The idea was to do only what actually had to be done (which was plenty), but to do each task contemplatively and deliberately. Some hearers who were already used to the idea of transformation of experience reported themselves as rather naturally accepting the suggestion that addressing Christmas cards can be an act of prayer for each recipient, for instance, and finding that a spiritual experience for the first time. What happens when the same approach is applied to deciding in what neighborhood one ought to live or spend one's money? Each shopping trip can become a way to work consciously to support minority businesses and thus enter the arena of social change first of all on the level of what one can do in daily life.

One of the chief motives for writing this book is to get preachers to be more specific, and therefore more useful in their preaching. At the same time, I do not want to give the impression that the preacher is to be the person with all the answers. I have already suggested that sermons invite the hearer to imagine and create. That can be pushed further by using the perfectly Biblical and creedal method of remembering the future.

The Rev. Charles Dodgson ("Lewis Carroll") put much of his wisdom into the mouths of his comic characters; in *Through the Looking Glass* the Queen remarks that "It's a poor sort of memory that works only backwards." We may not like having a fantasy novel remind us of this, but there is in that statement an important claim about the function of faith and hope. While prophets and apostles repeated promises about the future, it was the function of apocalyptic writers to remember the promised future in a way that was useful for their day. In an age of persecution, emperor worship, and the growing suspicion that Satan might in fact be the ultimate ruler of the world, John unveils *(apocaluptein)* a vision of the future in which terrible things indeed may occur, but one in which God is ultimately revealed as sovereign and in which Christ has gathered the redeemed to himself. Even the perennial problems of religion are transcended in the one lasting city, for in it there is no temple: that is the function of God and the Lamb. In their presence the faithful who have come through the great tribulation rejoice and have their rest and fulfillment. This vision of the future was and is comfort to those who struggle to be faithful in a fallen world, but it is more, it is an example of how Christians discover their resources.

Sermons should invite hearers to imagine the tasks and challenges they present as possible, just as this book asked you to imagine yourself as a great preacher before beginning its exploration of how preaching might be done. One way to do this is to look back from a desired future. Imagine with the hearers what it would be like to have accomplished a goal or realized a stage of growth, what it would look, feel and sound like. Give them a little silence to do that, and to relish their vision. This is what John is doing in presenting so early in his book the vision of the heavenly assembly in all its glory. Then ask: "What did you do to get there?" In John's apocalypse, the question is virtually the same, who are these and how did they get here? Note that it is John's "preacher" who asks him the question. On some deep level most of us know, at least in part, what it is we need to do, and it is part of the preacher's job to stir up the grace that is in us, to encourage us to find the words for the Spirit's sighs deep within us.

As a routine technique what I have just described would wear out quickly, and needs many variations. Nonetheless, it does illustrate something about how we preach power. The creeds celebrate an approach to life, one shaped by belief in the resurrection of the dead and the life of the world to come. The scriptures proclaim that the one who has gone before us holds the key to our history and destiny, and that we can be increasingly drawn into the power of that future, if we will remember the future and appropriate it. I offer here a small challenge. The radio comedian Fred Allen entitled the second volume of his autobiography *Treadmill to Oblivion,* and in three words encapsulated much of the work of the philosophers of two preceding generations. What three words can you imagine that just as powerfully express the Christian understanding of life lived toward the future we know in Christ? Look back on your life from your position near the throne of the Lamb, and you may be surprised at the answer you discover so naturally.

Have a good day—I have other plans.

Another important technique for communicating power is what some psychologists call a "reframe," putting things into a different context, transforming ourselves by transforming our understanding. Just as a painting appears different to us when it is displayed in a new frame, so our lives and the situations we face take on different meaning when we put them in different frames of understanding. The classic reframe is how we view the instrument of ignominious death, the cross: to the untrained eye shame or folly, but to us who are being saved it is the power and wisdom of God at work. Thus when Paul writes to the Philippians to "have this mind among you," he is asking them to perceive the world in a different frame, self-emptying *(kenosis)*. Norman Vincent Peale's positive thinkers and Robert Schuller's possibility thinkers may or may not know it, but their outlook is firmly grounded in the truth that as you believe, so shall it be unto you. Part of the work of the gospel is to retrain our perceptions, to ask us to see the world in a different way, having a new mind among us.

A small example can make the importance of one's "frame" clear. Here we return to our Jonahs, the habitually angry people. Several studies of angry people show that they themselves reinforce a negative view of life, maintaining in their heads a constant background chatter like those employed by athletic teams, but one of negative expectations. They are in almost constant rehearsal for disaster, and even contemplate revenge for wrongs they have not yet suffered. They then act out of their expectations in a way which does not always correspond to the way the world is in fact treating them. They go into encounters expecting bad results, and start punishing the "enemy" before any wrong has been done, a behavior which comes close to self-fulfilling prophecy. In therapy, these people have to learn to give themselves a new set of expectations about their environment.[37]

One does not need to be a chronically angry person to benefit from a reframe, however. Getting into a bad mood, or accentuating the negative is a trap into which anyone can fall, and one from which it is not at all hard to extricate oneself, as a story may illustrate.

Trying to explain academic life in a research university is as difficult as trying to explain the life of parish clergy. In some eyes you never really work; in others, usually those of your family, you never stop. I find that very often tangential or secondary responsibilities take me away from what I am currently paid to do, which is to think, publish, and teach. I confess that I am not beyond resenting this. The result of this state of affairs is that this book has been written in two-hour "chunks," that being time I could extract for it from my other responsibilities, and usually written quite early in the morning. Once at breakfast, when I was apparently entering the kitchen already anticipating a brutal day of what I assumed would be pointless and enervating bureaucratic detail, my wife Diana asked how the writing had been, and I replied that I had finished a certain section and was fairly content with it. "So you've already had a good day," she replied, knowing exactly what she was doing. She reframed my feelings about the day ahead, grounding them

---

[37] Gayle Rosellini and Mark Worden have reported on their work with angry people whose addiction (food, alcohol, gambling, shopping, etc.) served as buffers for anger in *Of Course You're Angry* (Minneapolis: Hazeldon, 1985), a book which has much to offer communicators and counselors in general.

in a sense of myself as already productive, instantly relaxing me to survive and contribute in a day for which I had other plans, plans to feel put upon and frustrated.

Christians have a double reframe constantly at hand. The life, death, and resurrection of Christ sum up what human existence is meant to be, transforming our understanding of love, power, and success. The future which we remember in Christ transforms our understanding of personal and global history: it is the most potent way we have of saying that life has meaning, that as Bishop Sheen used to say, life is worth living. Preachers have great opportunities to put our lives into the context of life with God, life in Christ, life led by the Spirit. To the baptized who celebrate the eucharist and can look back from the point of view of John's apocalypse, we have already had a good life.

As You are Doing

Do our sermons encourage people to continue doing what they already do well? Do they point out the seeds of greatness already springing up in and among members of your congregation, and then go on to cultivate them? Do they show hearers how the love that is already real in their lives can grow? In short, do sermons assume that we are preaching to already practicing Christians who are trying to be disciples, or would listeners get the impression that the preacher thinks that real religion is all news to them? Encouragement is a powerful tool in proclamation, because besides the reinforcement it gives to behavior, it makes the hearers more fully aware of the grace that is already at work in them. It can occasion thanksgiving.

It is important not to lie, particularly to people with whom you hope to have a productive relationship. The question for preachers is *which* truth or truths to tell. What one reinforces in people was part of the concern of the previous chapter: sermons that dwell on sin and guilt reinforce the notion in people that they understand themselves to be above all sinful and guilty. From such people one can expect little.

Getting into a new group is daunting: being a stranger in church is not easy for most people, even in a decade set aside for evangelism. In my current life I do a good bit of guest speaking in adult education forums. I have taken to arriving for such events in my normal secular working clothes rather than in a clerical collar. How I am treated as a stranger in these parishes, and not a particularly rich- or handsome-looking stranger, tells me a good deal about my audience and their common life. No matter how cold a place may be, there is usually one kind soul who will pity the stranger, and at least give directions to the coffee. This is a seed that must be watered. In such places I make a point of emphasizing how much I appreciate the help I received in finding my way. This comes from the fact that I have seen churches change the way newcomers are received when friendliness is frequently reinforced and valued in sermon and other communication, and always in the light of something that has happened. What I have come to call ethos shifts occur when what is already going on, no matter how minutely, is put in a frame which heightens its visibility and emphasizes its value. It is unlikely that scolding people into being friendly will work any more than handing them a balloon and telling them that they must now begin to "celebrate" will teach them joy. People respond to positive reinforcement and encouragement, and willingly act in accordance with their evolving self-perception. In theological language this partially explains why Christians are called such outrageous things as children of God, why they are bowed to, censed, washed and fed in their religious assemblies. Certainly part of the reason for this is that as creatures we are beloved of God and worthy of each other's love accordingly. Yet there is a much larger sense in which all these things, along with the embrace of the peace, model and reinforce an understanding of the life to which we are called, and into which we are encouraged to keep growing. This is the power of 1 Thess. 4:1: "We ask and urge you in the Lord Jesus, that as you learned from us how you ought to live and to please God, *as, in fact you are doing,* you do so more and more."

Rather than telling people that they do not care—few would be in church if that were really the case—a path to greater social action would be to find an expression of caring with which hearers can identify, and ask them to expand their love to the next level. Most people are carefully insulated from the realities of our national life, but when they do see them Christians will act. Thus in one parish the annual Thanksgiving food collection became a food pantry. Lay people delivering Christmas presents from the Sunday School to residents of one of their state's infamous welfare motels eventually had the parish making weekly trips with hot meals—and taking on the motel management about issues as basic as sanitation. Other ministries, including day care, grew from this, all without the overuse of "should." In written communication and in sermons, these efforts were always directly and specifically linked to compassion, to discipleship to Jesus, and to growth in the spiritual life. This was not always easy when the questions involved reallocating money, sharing space, and changing "turf" in the parish, and for some people these rough moments were times of personal growth. A few found themselves praying with intensity they would never have anticipated when neighborhood Yuppies baldly stated that they had come to the suburbs to escape the sight of poor people and wanted the church's day care closed down. Because grace rather than guilt was the motivator, members were not lost even when transition became complicated.

With most parishioners now "owning" the outreach projects in one way or another, the hard questions about systemic poverty had new meaning for them, became "our" concerns rather than issues for clergy or politicians. Parishioners sensed justice as part of the redemption of the world, rather than legal process. The issues before them were understood as God's issues, in which the parish had the privilege of a part to play. Their ministry was gift, not task.

Because the power really works, this is the place to reiterate the belief that the power, the how-to and with-whom section of the sermon, needs to be the best-prepared and most effective, and should be at least as long as the problem section, preferably longer if people are to move to new realizations and actions.

Conclusions

The sermon's conclusion is a kind of a paradox. Its function is to provide closure to something which is not to end at that moment. That is, if a sermon has identified an important issue and brought to bear the resources of the faith, listeners should feel that something is just beginning or increasing in their lives. The conclusion should not have the effect of the dentist's whipping away the paper bib and returning the chair to its upright position: we feel that we are "done," and don't have to think about this again for six months.

In general, the conclusion should leave the hearer with a clear idea of what is to be done, and puts that idea in a positive "frame." The positive frame will help make the sermon's goal seem both attainable and desirable. Thus the conclusion not infrequently employs a special kind of "leading," one usually called "future pacing," one which already has the hearer anticipating and somewhat rehearsed for the moment when the sermon's message will go into action. How might the steward-ship sermon which has been lurking in the last two chapters end? Given our previously stipulated crowd of Yuppies bent on self-fulfillment, it might end as follows:

> So when you sit down to write your checks this week, you may be surprised at how easily you have come to see your pen and checkbook in a new way. More than anything else they may appear to be the tools of your caring for your family, your community, and for all of God's creation. They become instruments of willing discipleship. Using their power well this week may be one of the most reli-gious—and fulfilling—things you do for yourself.

I chose to end that paragraph with "for yourself" because of the way our hypothetical audience has been postulated, and to show how complex theological truths, in this case self-giving as the path to fulfillment, can be stated compactly. The last word of the sermon is very important, perhaps more important than the last sentence of which it is a part. The last word should come as close as possible to leaving people in a positive, ready-to-go state. A student once ended a very good sermon on the Prodigal Son with an exhortation that we "remember that we are invited to a party whenever we come to ourselves and seek forgiveness of our sins." When asked about the last sentence, some class mem-bers focussed on "party," which they found less powerful than "feast" or "banquet," but several of them thought that ending the sermon with "our sins" was in truth giving the "last word" to words very heavy with symbolic freight which detracted from the preacher's main point. The student thought this over for a while and tried this: "In a story full of unexpected moments, the greatest of all is the discovery that when we turn from our sins, what we come to is a feast—a feast we attend still filled with the warmth of the Father's embrace." His second ending had a much better effect on the class, and on how they remembered the rest of the sermon.

We have now explored generally and with depth in some places the production of a three-P sermon, a model which can be a staple of homiletical diet. It can, when thoroughly learned, work far better than canned sermon starters for those times when sermons must be improvised, because by continually asking its three questions, what are we called to (Point), how must we change (Problem), and how can this be done (Power), we form habits of mind for preaching and for sorting and storing our own experiences in that general and essential preparation for preaching which goes by the name of living.

8. Writing

I must begin by admitting that if you have followed all of the steps described in the preceding chapters and have some speaking talent, you will be able to preach fairly well from your outline. If you have a good memory for structure, and are comfortable with your audience, you will probably be able to get through a sermon without any paper at all. To do this you will need to practice the sermon several times mentally, but you will not need to have a complete text.

Nonetheless, there are good reasons for writing out a sermon whenever possible. These reasons do not contradict or even question the indisputable fact that when we preach without paper in front of us our communication seems freer and livelier, and that people experience us as talking with them directly. Our discussion of delivery techniques explores ways to do that whether paper is present or not. Certainly most of us have had moments of intense clarity (and adrenalin) when we threw away our notes and extemporaneously delivered ourselves of what someone told us was "the best sermon I ever heard." There is no reason to doubt that the Spirit can take charge of the preaching event in such a way; there is every reason not to presume upon such intervention.

The first and most important reason to write sermons is that writing makes us exact, gives us the opportunity to clarify and hone our thinking. Just as there are a very few people who can do a London *Times* crossword puzzle in their heads, there may well be a few people who can plan where each paragraph and sentence of a sermon will go without writing, and then remember it all for delivery. I am not one of them, and have not met any of them in the ranks of parish preachers. To say what we want to say and to say it the way we mean it takes work, takes writing and revising. To write it out means to wrestle with the Spirit, to wrestle with ideas and their expression, to get the sermon so that it feels, sounds, and looks right to the preacher before it is launched from the pulpit. To write the sermon is to take every word of it seriously.

My observation of colleagues leads me to believe that preachers develop very slowly, if at all, as either theologians or homilists, unless they write most of their sermons. As preachers we are concerned to make accurate and helpful connections between theology and life, and our words need to be carefully placed. It is only by writing that we really come to know our own minds and order their content.

The written sermon gives control over the expression of personal strengths. What is obvious or feels right to us needs to be explained to others who do not share our experience or insight. Writing also keeps our personal inclinations in check. For instance, irony, delicious as it is, almost always needs to be stripped from the text, because it gives double messages to some listeners and confuses and alienates others. The written sermon has fewer of the asides which extemporaneous preachers sometimes come to regret.

The written sermon also teaches you things you may not at first wish to know about yourself. Besides the obvious control it provides over cliché and redundancy, encountering a manuscript for many is the point at which they hear themselves tell their own story. Extemporaneous speakers cannot avoid telling their own stories. John Savage tells of an assistant minister who worked for a "star" in a big parish, apparently quite happily. However, the assistant began a sermon on the account of Peter and Andrew this way, and by all reports in all innocence:

Our gospel today tells us the story of two brothers. One quietly did all the work, and the other was the public figure who got all the glory and to whom history gave all the credit.

Had the curate written that out and come back to it a day later and asked himself what his telling of the biblical story revealed about his own story, he would have realized that he had endangered more than the effectiveness of his sermon.

Most of the argument of this book has been to urge you to appropriate and use your experience in preparing sermons. The warning here is that by writing we are in a position to use and appropriate our experience consciously and helpfully. By not writing we put ourselves in the position where that experience will appear anyway, unconsciously and perhaps not helpfully.

Writing gives us the chance to struggle with the hardest part of the sermon, providing resources for Christian living. Writing invites us to be concrete and specific, will not let us get away with generalizations which appear sufficient in an outline but in a manuscript appear stale, flat, and unprofitable.

In general, the more time one puts into construction, the better the finished project. Confidence in delivery comes from knowing and believing in what one has to say, and the writer is in the best position to have such confidence. Writing a sermon manuscript requires about three hours of concentration. Having written it on Friday and revised it on Saturday, the total comes up to five hours. That investment is considerable, but what one gains is eight hours of uninterrupted sleep on Saturday night and the ability to be focussed and present to the people who are in church on Sunday.

A friend at General Seminary turned in a paper, which came back with a number of comments, including "you write easily." The student wrote back, "No, it reads easily." Sermons should be listened to easily. For most of us that goal can be attained only by writing, writing hard.

A Script

What one is writing must be grasped clearly in mind. Most of us when confronted by a keyboard or legal pad shift into "term paper mode," and become somewhat formal, careful, and abstract. When setting out to write a sermon it is important to remember that you are not writing an essay for posterity or even for the parish newsletter. You are writing a script for oral presentation. If the sermon is to be printed later, revise it for publication after it has had its life as a script.

Sit down with your outline and turn its concepts into sentences. Imagine how you speak each sentence or paragraph before writing it. Most of us speak an interesting mixture of long and short sentences, and sometimes employ "periodic sentences" which join several thoughts into one flow. The sermons of Peter Marshall are famous for being written in what usually looks like poetry. Whether or not they were poems, he did write his sermons in the way he spoke, in sense lines rather than sentences, and sometimes went on for a while without a complete stop. No one looking at those manuscripts and imagining what they sounded like can doubt that they were sermons, not essays. Write a script for yourself as you sound when addressing a group. Use the dash where necessary to approximate your speech—the way you actually talk.

Writing Difficulties

People sometimes freeze up when they try to write. Most universities have therapy groups for doctoral students who have done their research but cannot write a dissertation. Few of us have escaped the experience of staring at a screen or a piece of paper, unable to think of a good opening sentence.

When you are "stuck," because you cannot get the right sentence or cannot get the paragraph you are working on to say what you want it to, you must take steps to eliminate frustration. Otherwise you will walk away from the project. What has worked for me is to say to myself "just get it written, and revise later" and plunge on. Taking away the pressure of getting each part just right before forging ahead allows me to finish a draft which I can vigorously revise later on. Not having to be right now sometimes also allows me to be creative instead.

Sometimes that technique of just pushing on does not work for me. On those occasions the block almost always means that I have not thought through what I am writing—or that on some deep level I do not believe it. I have learned to value such "blocks" and take them as signals to go back to the recliner and think things through again.

Sometimes students have responded well to a little coaching. "Tell me your main idea," "Tell me why it matters," "When did you see it in action?" These questions and others related to problem and power usually get the student to express the heart of the sermon. Then it is possible to say "Just write that down, and revise it later." The "later" is added to relieve the pressure of getting it right the first time.

Some people have responded to simple reframes. Have you noticed that in the sciences people "write up" their research, but in the humanities they "write down" their ideas? For reasons I do not fully understand, asking people to shift these metaphors sometimes helps break them free from blockage, and divinity students quite happily go to "write up" sermons they were unable to write "down." People who report the feeling of emotional blocks in sermons have found it helpful to "write it out," with an image of poets and musicians in mind.

Some people have found it helpful to install a mental "switch" which puts them into a resourceful state. They are asked to close their eyes and relax, then to recall a time when they wrote clearly and well, a time when they knew what they wanted to say, and said it well. They are asked to hold their memory of that time, what it felt like, what they saw, what they heard, even any aromas they may recall. As the experience peaks (this is evident from shifts in posture, skin color, and breathing) they are told to press their left thumb and forefinger together to "anchor" that experience. The subject of conversation is changed for a few minutes, and then we test the anchor. Pressing the thumb and forefinger together again almost always brings back the emotional experience of knowing what to say and how to say it. Students find this a helpful preparation for test-taking as well. I use it before meetings.[38]

Another technique has already been introduced in terms

---

[38] This is a basic technique developed by Grinder and Bandler, and is discussed in many of their works, including *Trance Formations,* cited in Chapter Five.

of remembering the future. Ask a frustrated writer to imagine having completed the sermon, to feel the satisfaction of having done the job well; let the writer thoroughly experience success. Then ask "What did you do to get it written?" Most people will know.

Time Is Tight

Sometimes sermons cannot be written completely. The realities of parish life sometimes take one's time away. When it is not possible to write the whole sermon, and only one part can be written, that part should be the conclusion. The trouble with most sermons extemporized from an outline is that the preacher is so obviously struggling for an ending that the audience tunes out or feels vicariously embarrassed. If that paragraph has been written, the most awkward part of improvised sermons can be mended. If there is more time, an effective introduction should be written next. Then power can be written. Last of all attend to the problem, which is what most preachers are best at defining on the fly.

Beyond Pronouns: Inclusive Language

The goal of our preaching is to help all Christians reach full maturity. We seek this for their own sake, for the sake of the church, and for the care of the world. This is why sermons are illustrated with enlightening and encouraging stories of Christians living and dead. Merely from a results-oriented viewpoint then, it is important that the illustrations we choose and the language we use not give any members of the assembly the impression that their role is limited artificially: this would defeat the point of our preaching. Put another way, we seek to preach in a way that encourages all members to become everything that God has created them to be, and to do all that they are called to do.

St. Paul's attempt to be everything to everyone is a reminder that the needs of the audience control the form our proclamation of Christ needs to take. Our time is one in which people have been made aware that much of traditional religious discourse exalts men and minimizes women, and that most of it ignores or debases non-Europeans. It is a serious mistake not to preach to people's ears the way they are, demanding that hearers decode the preacher by standards other than their own. It simply asks too much of them both to translate and meditate on a sermon at once. If we had an audience which understood French, would we preach in German? Hardly. The language of the sermon should be as close as we can come to language which all listeners can readily hear without needing special filters.

A commonly imposed filter is "But everyone knows that the masculine pronoun really includes the feminine." The reality of our time is that for good or ill most people no longer perceive the masculine as including the feminine.

It is necessary then that our language be inclusive of men and women of all backgrounds. Doing this is not always easy, because our language has not developed with this in mind. Crude circumlocutions repel hearers, and worse, they draw attention to themselves, thus defeating their purpose. "Sacraments are effective signs of God's self-giving of God's self to God's people" was written by a tenured professor at a major university, and demonstrates the worst kind of inclusive language: it is crude and asks people to notice it, without drawing anyone into its content. In learning to write English in a way that draws everyone into the discourse we find another reason to write our sermons completely. We want to struggle with the words to make them bear the message without dwelling on its vehicle. *The whole point of inclusive language is that it not be noticed.* Language is inclusive when it is transparent and engages all listeners naturally in its content.[39]

This is why the issue is larger than (but not exclusive of) considering how white male preachers cease to exclude women and ethnic minorities, and it is certainly much larger than pronouns. For the moment, we continue with the issue of women as our chief example.

This is a point to emphasize another rule of writing: I think that we ought never to use stories which give private data about people, especially our family members, without their permission. People do not expect their confidences to become sermon illustrations, no matter how harmless we may think they are. A way to make your trustworthiness clear in a sermon is to preface a story with something like "this came up recently, and I have permission to tell you this story."

I have permission to tell you this story. My daughter has a great, possibly prodigious, aptitude for mathematics, and in her school "Math Olympiads" has usually been at least school champion. When we moved to New Haven, she encountered a culture in which the message to her was explicit in both words and actions: young women are not supposed to do well

---

[39] The best combination of theory and practical advice currently on the market is probably Rosalie Maggio, *The Nonsexist Word Finder. A Dictionary of Gender-free Usage* (Boston: Beacon Press, 1988). The book deliberately includes religion in the areas it addresses. Maggio shares my belief that inclusive English need not be bad English, and has put in the hours to create a resource for writers. Her book contains a dictionary of 500 entries, giving alternatives to problem words. In the lexicon she delivers more than she promises, as racial and ethnic concerns are taken up along with gender issues. The appendices include reprints of key articles, including Dorothy Sayers now-classic "Are Women Human?" For those who do not think theological language needs attention the article "Is God Purple?" is required reading.

in math here—math is male country. The day that she, unaware of this culture, did significantly better than any boy on the first math test of the year, boys were verbally abusive and girls rejected her as not knowing her place and upsetting the social ecology. The emotional impact of the experience and the parenting issues it raised hardly need explication here. Eventually, however, she determined to be who she is, and has in fact begun to change the attitudes of her peer group and male teachers, and now has something of a friend in the young man who used to be the math champ. She happens to have a family and church environment which encourages women to be themselves. What if she did not? Can America, which produces only a tiny fraction of the mathematics doctorates it needs, afford to lose half of its potential pool?

In the church the same question should be about all those not conventionally portrayed as powerful. How many African-American or Asian-American children in mainline denominations get a religious formation which gives them images or stories of powerful and effective Christians of their race with whom to identify? Can the church afford to lose all the high-power potential disciples who do not happen to be white men? Furthermore, can we bear the responsibility of, as one person put it, killing the souls of those outside the conventional power structure?

Obviously not. The responsibility is not just to cease to discriminate *against* women and racial minorities. There is a positive duty as well: *preachers need to select images and illustrations which are both remedial and reconstructive of our general attitude.* If members of racial minorities are predominantly portrayed as people in a weak position who need the help of the majority culture, unhealthy stereotypes are reinforced, often with the best of intentions. There is clear need, for the sake of the marginalized and also for the sake of members of the group in power, that images and illustrations in sermons portray healthy creative disciples of Jesus of all sorts and conditions, and do so consistently.

Thus men must not put off preaching from the examples of women, leaving that to women preachers. Similarly, white preachers must not succumb to the idea that preaching from the stories of strong black people is somehow "black property," as one listener put it. One of my African-American students quite wisely insisted that at our chapel's Martin Luther King celebrations, if King is to be owned by the whole church, the preacher should be anyone but a black a good deal of the time.

Similarly, women ought not be portrayed as appendages of men. Nothing is more irritating than well-intentioned extemporaneous emendations of Eucharistic Prayer "C" in the Book of Common Prayer from "God of Abraham, Isaac, and Jacob" to "God of Abraham and Sarah," and so on. As well-meaning and defensible as the alteration is, a correction would make its point better if it included women whose stories are not remembered primarily in conjunction with their husbands. "God of Abraham, Isaac, and Jacob; God of Deborah, Ruth, and Esther" seems to be a happier solution for this reason. In sermons it is similarly important to portray racial minorities, women, and other marginalized people acting on their own, and doing so for the benefit of all.

Thus it is fair to ask some questions. Do handicapped persons appear in our sermons only as those for whom the vestry is asked to build ramps? Do women always appear as passive, or as always nurturing? Do we ever mention well-known members of minorities in contexts other than those which refer to their minority identity? The real issue of inclusivity is theological: can we portray images which show how powerfully the Spirit works in all flesh? Can our sermons quietly and consistently portray men and women of all races and ethnicity as full citizens in

God's realm? Being careful to do that, and to do it all of the time, has a greater cumulative effect than occasional sermons which directly relate to those issues. Such sermons certainly ought to be preached, but their validity and effectiveness is largely created by what happens in sermons which do not happen to be about those issues. The contemporary preacher then has a duty to seek illustrations which correct an evil situation and provide all hearers with a fuller and richer vision of humanity in Christ.

But the Bible Says . . .

In all of this, the preacher is free from the problems which face the editor of liturgical texts and the translator of scripture. The liturgical editor has a tremendous responsibility to verbal tradition for great and good cause. The biblical translator has a primary duty to present what the text says in such a way that we can hear the ancient voices with precision.

Preaching, however, is always meant to paraphrase, it is meant to put ancient ideas into modern words. The preacher has the freedom, arguably the duty, without "changing the Bible," to relate its content faithfully in a way that modern ears can hear, and with images and illustrations that make clear that our churches are houses of prayer for all people and that indeed God shows no partiality (Acts 10:34).

"Sex" is a Latin word which means division, and it implies incompleteness, naming that which is only one part of a set or group. Thus there is the necessary paradox in Christian orthodoxy that "God the Father" cannot be male, that God is neither "he" nor "she." Human language does not have a convenient way of expressing this truth because it is outside of our ordinary experience, and today's preacher must struggle to express that truth creatively and constructively. This is not the time to abandon or re-write the creeds. It is not time to pretend that a religion based in history can survive without reference to individuals or specific events. However, it is a time to tell people about God in such a way that the whole Biblical revelation is presented, and God presented as the source of all being, whose image both men and women can detect in themselves and cherish in each other. This cannot be a treatise on religious language, but the preacher has in writing a sermon the opportunity and challenge to see that the meaning of specific events is preached in a way which invites all hearers to enter and experience the meaning of that sacred history.

Writer's Tools

Since the Middle Ages there have been helps for preachers. On the eve of the Reformation there were canned sermon collections such as *Sermons That Preach Themselves*, and collections of illustrations and funny stories for preachers to use in the pulpit. The Reformation interest in preaching increased the number and variety of homiletical resources available. Our day sees everything from collections of anecdotes to resources for sermon writing to outlines to entire sets of sermons geared to the church year.

Each of those resources has value, provided they pass through preachers' souls, and what comes out of their mouths is in some sense their own. In the last few months, as I have discussed this project with lay leaders met on my travels, there have been two consistent observations among the many things they have to say about preaching. The first is that it is unsettling for them when the preacher is unprepared and obviously extemporizing. What troubles them more is when they suspect that the preacher uses canned sermons, and sounds like someone else.

When queried about this, what offends these lay people is not so much the question of professional ethics or laziness, although both suspicions were ventilated, but their feeling of being let down by someone they wish to trust. Pressed further, they are themselves not as much concerned with elegance as with hearing a sermon which they can identify as their spiritual leader's honest attempt to deal with scripture and life. I asked some of them if they ever considered even hinting at these things to the preacher. Almost none of them had, so these conversations are reported here as a reminder that people are not easily fooled, and can in fact tell if we have not invested ourselves in what we preach.

How does one use prepackaged homiletical material? In the first place, it is probably a very good idea for preachers to read or listen to the sermons of others. Since most preachers are busy every Sunday, the normal way to do this is through books and tapes. Each week the mail delivers to your church at least half a dozen opportunities to purchase this material; if you are not on the church staff, you might ask the pastor or secretary to save you some of the "junk mail." When studying these sermons, it is helpful to look for how other preachers understand the scriptures, how they make connections to contemporary life, and how they structure and word their sermons. Someone who takes preaching seriously might well study two sermons a week from a variety of sources.

Beyond that, such packages have immediate use. Homily services come in many forms. A service such as the National Catholic Reporter's *Celebration* is valuable because it provides resources for sermon, music, bulletin, and educational programs in a coordinated way that suggests a parish intentionally living the liturgical year together. It provides exegesis of the lessons, homiletical questions and resources, specimen prayers of the people, and a model homily. The model homilies are just that:

something to stimulate thinking. There are also supplementary "story sermons" and materials for children. Other Roman Catholic and Lutheran groups provide similar packages.

Using materials of this kind gives the preacher something to think about, suggests paths to search in personal memory, and sometimes provides a point of view from which Sunday's sermon can differ! It is a way for preachers to be in stimulating conversation with their colleagues.

A Commonplace Book

Valuable as they are, a limitation of homily services, books of sermon illustrations and books of quotations (religious or otherwise), is that often one has little idea of what they are supposed to mean, how they made sense in someone else's pattern of selection. A second problem is even greater. Such selections have not been thought through, felt through, or lived through by you, the preacher, and thus their meaning and emotional impact may remain undisclosed to you. Before directly using any of these resources, like any truth we preach, their message must have been understood and processed internally by the preacher.

The fact is that the best bank of sermon illustrations is your own experience remembered and considered. There is something to be said to noting down your own experiences, reading, and observations, and keeping them in an informal scrapbook, usually called a commonplace book. Mine, now in several spiral bound volumes with the most recent additions spinning on a hard disk, contain items as varied as cartoons, observations upon travelling abroad, and the dying words of a parishioner, with quotations from many sources in between. I am constitutionally incapable of keeping a diary and have no discipline about what goes into the commonplace book or when.

I only note things down when they make such an impression on me that I want to remember them and how I reacted to them. Into it go ideas and fragments for sermons, notes transferred from my pocket datebook, jottings on theater programs and other scraps of paper. Occasionally an event or conversation will provoke a line or a page of reflection, or just be recorded for later consideration.

Some teachers tell students not to bother writing any of this down because they will not remember why they recorded it. It is probably safer simply to say that if you do not profit from writing things down, don't. However, if you do, and are not certain that you will remember why you did so, adding just a line about how you connect or react to them makes the record more valuable.

It is possible that you may never quote most of your jottings directly. Nonetheless, they do provide a storehouse of ideas and observations that may provoke your own thinking. My collection is some twenty years old now, and I find fascinating what seemed important to me that many years ago. How much has changed is nearly as interesting as how much has remained near the center of my concerns.

As in the Beginning

It is important to recall the point made earlier. The work of writing will be experienced differently when done in and as prayer. It is well known that J. S. Bach's working manuscripts began with INJ (in the name of Jesus) at the top and ended SDG (to God alone be the glory). Such a discipline may help to make the crafting of each sermon the way in which one acts the prayer, "God, I put myself at your disposal."

9. Revision

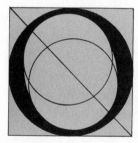ne professor of another generation urged that sermons be written in pencil, so that nothing in them would strike their authors as permanent. He believed that this would make the task of revision psychologically easier. The advent of electronic word processing has made his desire an institution: most of us who use such machines revise both as we write and after a draft is complete.

It is important to let time pass between writing and serious revision. As someone caught up in the internal logic (and perhaps unstated presuppositions) of the sermon, the writer just laying down the pen or pushing the "save" button is not in a good position to test the sermon. The writer who has just put a great deal of self into a manuscript may be unable to see its faults—or in some cases its virtues. Let the manuscript sit over night and come back to it.

When returning to the manuscript, read the whole thing through before changing anything (this means printing it out, rather than working with a screen-full at a time). Questions might be noted in the margin, but the reviser needs to attend to the forest before mending trees.

It helps to ask first, what is the overall feeling tone of this sermon? Is there anything in it, particularly in the "problem" parts, that suggests that I do not value and respect the hearer as a person? Have I dropped any bombs in this sermon which have so much emotional impact that they need to be addressed in supplementary or alternative events? Are the people addressed in this sermon the people to whom it is to be delivered? Are the sermon's issues real for that audience?

We can then ask how God is presented: is any of my crankiness projected onto God? When God's judgment, warnings, or law are presented, are they done so in a way that makes it clear that this is the same God whom we know as love?

Having examined the forest, it seems appropriate at this point to look at some of the larger trees. Is the "power" part of the sermon as compelling as the rest of the manuscript? What does God actually do or provide to encourage and help the listener appropriate and follow through on the Point?

Then I have learned to ask how the sermon deals with or appropriates the gifts of the day's lessons and our location in the liturgical year. I confess here with some embarrassment how often a re-reading of the propers at this point has filled gaping holes in my sermons or provided power I was not able to detect until I worked the sermon through a first draft. In fact, for me, if there is time for only one serious effort at revision, I re-read the lessons.

Then one might look at the central illustration in each part of the sermon. Is it sufficient or does it require auxiliary illustrations? Conversely, are the illustrations so numerous as to distract the hearer from the flow or point of the sermon? Do the illustrations invite all listeners to enter the ideas they represent?

Does the sermon address all the questions or issues raised in the introduction, at least by dealing with the fact that we may not know the answer?

Finally, it is good to ask if *anything* in this sermon reinforces racism, sexism, or denominational triumphalism, either by omission or commission.

At this point the rest of the trees can be tended. This is where individual words and phrases are fine-tuned, expressions "punched up," grammar checked, and our habitual recourse to split infinitives healed.

English is a hybrid language. As a consequence, each Latin-French word in our vocabulary usually has a Saxon equivalent.[40] The former are often polysyllabic and relatively abstract, while the latter are often monosyllabic and more concrete. It is useful to see how the impact of the sermon changes when polysyllabic and abstract locutions are exchanged for words short and real. The abstract gives the hearer distance from the idea, the concrete brings it near. When I find a nest of abstractions in a sermon on which I am working, I usually write "p.p." (polysyllabic perversity) in the margin and come back to think it through more clearly. Upon such reexamination I often find that the abstract language appeared because I had not made real connection between the idea and life.

Similarly, it is useful to look for religious code, words which require special knowledge on the hearer's part. These come in two kinds. The first is the technical language of theology. There is no excuse for preachers flashing their technical

---

[40] See William Safire, *On Language* (New York: Times Books, 1980). Safire illustrates his very similar point by translating the short and direct language of the Gettysburg Address into the language of today's deep thinkers who have gathered because "a proposal has been made to inter non-viable casualties" in the battlefield.

vocabulary in sermons. Doing so can be a kind of boasting which creates a division between preacher and hearer or else to some ears it suggests personal insecurity: in either case the sermon suffers from decreased effectiveness. It is particularly unhelpful to use foreign words in sermons. More than anything, except beginning "when I was completing my Rhodes scholarship . . .," such expressions unhelpfully focus attention on the preacher's erudition rather than on the message. For instance, it is quite possible to preach an Advent sermon on the biblical view of time without ever mentioning *kairos* or *chronos,* yet few new preachers can resist this temptation. Having to make the distinction between undifferentiated time and the right time in the hearer's language produces a much more useful sermon. This is true because the preacher must grasp for examples that the congregation will readily accept based on their experience rather than the preacher's say-so. One can have a successful and effective preaching career and never mention words such as eschatological, prolepsis, *Heilsgeschicte,* inculturation, paranesis, and even anamnesis, although one will certainly convey the meanings they represent. Just as surely, the technical vocabulary of the social sciences should be avoided. Sermons certainly and unavoidably teach. After all, they explore a new reality, but they do not draw attention to the fact that they do so.

This is not to suggest that one speaks to an assembly of Christian adults as though the preacher were Mr. Rogers addressing a television audience still in early childhood. Sometimes technical terms need to be introduced because they are the best or the only words for the concept the preacher explores; this is not often the case, however. The language of sermons should not deflect the audience's attention from the things of life, life lived with God. When we avoid theological abstractions and the defense systems that technical vocabulary invokes, we get more easily to our real target, the point where heart and brain meet.

The sermons of Paul Tillich never remind one of the professor writing a systematic theology. They connect profound truth with real life. In the same vein, the best, and perhaps only good, sermon I have heard on the Trinity was preached by a highly sophisticated student who knew her theology well enough to explain it in terms that were the words of life, intimacy, and community of will, all key aspects of the doctrine. She preached on the Trinity as though it were good news, not a painful duty. When she was through we cared, we knew again that God mattered, and that what we can know of God's being is key to understanding our own.

A more dangerous kind of code consists of the religious words that everybody thinks they understand. A strong case can be made for not using nouns like love, forgiveness, grace, stewardship, sacrament, and apostolic ministry in sermons, and using in their place verbs which describe what happens in the actions flash-frozen in such nouns. At the very least these terms need to be defined when used. This is true because everybody thinks they know what these words mean, and yet people are far from agreed on what the meaning might be. For instance, to some the word forgiveness brings with it the memory of being very tentatively let off the hook, being put on probation by someone who would rather punish them. For others it means getting away with something once again because they said they were sorry. For others it is the basic condition of a life of spiritual indolence. None of these meanings is appropriate to Christianity, but they cannot be challenged unless the concept is explained in its gospel terms. A sermon devoted to the topic would go into detail, but one in which the term was brought up in a less central way might well insert an explanation, such as "forgiveness, the warm embrace we find when we return to God," or, more conceptually framed, "forgiveness, God's restoring the relationship we damage through sin." It seems especially important on those occasions when most of the congregation are not active church members to be clear about the meaning of religious language and the vocabulary of our particular subculture. Ezra Pound once observed that the essence of style is in verbs, not adjectives. "God is good" is not a particularly helpful observation, and to some hearers may be quite debatable. What God did and does demands our attention.

On a high level of revision, if there is time, it is worth it to check for the dominance of one representational system, those sorting techniques discussed in Chapter Six. Is my language predominantly visual? Can I change any of it to auditory or kinesthetic language to include more of the congregation?

These repairs made, a final read through, perhaps out loud, gives the preacher the chance to ask, "Is this what I really want to say?" When the answer is yes, revision is done. Perhaps in beginning years one asks a spouse or significant other for reflections on the manuscript at this point, and the reassurances and help those people give are valuable. Nonetheless, the final test needs to be whether the sermon sounds and feels right to the one who must preach it, whether it is a sermon which seems appropriate and helpful to the gathering of the preacher's brothers and sisters at the Lord's table.

10. Delivery

ermons as deeply felt and carefully constructed as those which we have been considering deserve not to be lost in delivery. In fact, they deserve to be delivered in such a way that we in the congregation experience the speaker as engaging, committed to the message, and worthy of trust when we consider the very important topics which the sermon addresses. Many a good sermon has failed because of bad delivery, and some quite ordinary ones have had their full effect because good delivery skills were employed.

In our culture, conditioned to see "talking heads" on television and thirty-foot tall heros on movie screens, preachers ideally stand as close to the congregation as is appropriate to the space. That appropriateness is defined by the need for everyone to be able to see and hear, which means that in a large room the preacher needs a platform or pulpit.

Ideally preachers know their sermons well enough to preach without reference to notes, so that all of their attention and energy can be devoted to engaging the listeners. Nonetheless, we are all in different stages of the journey to ideal delivery, and sometimes most of us do need paper in front of us. This chapter discusses a variety of delivery techniques appropriate to a variety of circumstances.

The Eye-Mouth Rule

Next to being heard, the most important part of effective delivery is eye contact. Especially in our culture, the degree of mutuality, honesty, and intimacy in a relationship is expressed and perceived through giving or withholding eye contact. Described below are four strategies for getting the sermon out. They range from a technique for reading a manuscript to a totally paperless delivery. All of them assume one thing: the preacher's mouth is never moving unless there is eye contact with listeners. Preachers talk to people, not to their manuscripts. We are seeking precisely the opposite effect of that achieved by good reading of the scriptures in the liturgy. There the reader seldom looks up, and deliberately avoids lots of eye contact with the congregation, because the goal in reading the lessons is to draw everyone's attention to the written word and keep that attention focussed on the book, which is the real speaker. Thus the reader's eyes, kept on the book, draw us to the message. The sermon, on the other hand, is meant to be a contemporary spoken word, heart speaking to heart, so the preacher's eyes serve to draw us into that transaction, which is between us in the here and the now.

Again, a large part of the reason for this is cultural. In mainstream America, sincerity is indicated to a great degree by eye contact. "Look me in the eye when you say that." Your eyes steadily focussed on those of the listener indicate trustworthiness. Eyes which look away or shift rapidly are usually taken as signs of untrustworthiness. Speakers who do not look at their audiences are perceived to be uninterested or "too intellectual."

Eyes are very small, yet our sensitivity to them is acute: we can tell across a large room if someone is looking at us, has "caught our eye." The general rule for preaching, then, is *keep contact with one pair of eyes for each thought you express.* This thought may be a sentence, or part of a long one. The eyes should move naturally from one side of the room to another, changing their depth of focus and rhythm of movement so as not to be predictable or monotonous. Only rarely does one speak to the back wall or with unfocussed eyes to people in general (again, this latter is appropriate to some kinds of liturgical speech, such as the eucharistic dialogue, where a more general effect is sought). The listener's visual acuity and spatial perception are sharper than we may think: the hearer knows when we are engaging no one, everyone, someone, or ourselves. By practicing eye contact and disciplining ourselves to look at someone in each area of the congregation we can insure that even in large congregations, each person can feel addressed fairly directly. In a large church, those with whom you may not be able to make individual eye contact will still respond well to a preacher whom they perceive as present to the people in the room.[41] Avoid talking to paper.

---

[41] The bibliography on this point is more than ample, thanks largely to the money corporations have spent on research and in training sales and managerial personnel in effective speech. A theoretical base for concepts presented in this chapter can be found in the works on communication cited in previous chapters, and more technically in Andrew Ellis, *The Psychology of Language and Communication* (London: Weidenfield and Nicolson, 1986) and Robert Landers, *Cognitive Foundations of Calculated Speech* (Albany: State University of New York Press, 1987). Practical help may be gotten in more depth in Michael Kenny's manual for Eastman Kodak employees, *Presenting Yourself* (New York: Wiley, 1982).

They shall be like trees, planted

When we lived in another state a friend was "shopping" for a church in our area, so I recommended one where I knew the rector to be a caring and responsible type of about the same disposition and values as my friend. I encountered her some time later and was surprized to learn that she had joined another parish, one which was not oriented toward the constituency of which she seemed to be a part. When I asked if she had been to St. X., she replied, and I quote her exactly, "the sermons made me want to throw up."

It turned out that she meant that quite literally. She has motion sickness of the common type induced by instability of visual horizon—the sort that causes some people to get sick if they try to read in a car. They can drive for hours without illness because their eyes and the balancing equipment in their middle ear are giving their brains the same information about their relationship to the environment. Give them the kind of perfectly straight line a book asks them to focus on, however, and things change. The visual data gives the brain messages of calm stability, while their bodies report that they are rocking and moving, and the resulting confusion means nausea for that part of the population who get motion sick easily. In extreme cases it can happen to anyone, particularly those deprived of any true horizon line, a fact which explains the little bags in the back of airplane seats. When my friend visited the church I had recommended she encountered one staff member whose nervousness expressed itself as he constantly and pointlessly paced the center aisle while preaching. He was almost always in motion, going back and forth across the fairly narrow space which a nave aisle is, and pacing up and down at the same time. Many people in the congregation simply looked away—my friend felt both fascinated and increasingly queasy. The next week another member of the clergy team preached. Many preachers and speakers, unconsciously recalling the cradle, their parents' arms, and perhaps even their nine-month's cushioned journey in a sea of amniotic fluid, rock themselves back and forth on their heels when nervousness strikes. This preacher rocked herself both in preaching and in officiating at the altar: her liturgical ministry was like a sea voyage. Half way through the sermon my friend made a dash for the restroom, and then went out the church door for the last time.

These visually distracting habits drove my friend from that church. Her story is an extreme case, and relates to an unusual set of circumstances. What is more interesting than entertaining about it is the fact that in the parish in question the behaviors just described routinely caused many listeners simply to look away from the preacher, or otherwise to tune out. It must have been very perplexing to that particular pair of clergy to wonder why so many in their congregation did not look at them when they preached. It may even, as subsequent history of that parish suggests, have been somewhat demoralizing to them.

This extreme example points out the truth that if we want good eye contact with people, we must not be visually distracting ourselves. We ought not encourage them to look away. Therefore, in preaching *movement should always have a purpose.* Random shifting about is in our culture a sign of unease, nervousness, unreliability, lack of purpose, and often a very clear indication that the speaker does not know what to say or do next. The preacher who tries to increase effectiveness by wandering the aisles is only half right. We do value proximity. We do not value vagrancy. The first skill taught to people who take expensive executive communication courses on Madison Avenue is how to stand still. Preaching in the nave is highly effective in groups small enough to see and hear the preacher. I also find the close proximity to the congregation stimulating and supportive to me when preaching. But again, freedom from the pulpit is not freedom to wander: it is freedom to move with purpose. I find it helpful to move deliberately as the structure of the sermon does. Particularly when introducing a new idea or suggesting change to a new and better reality, I move, usually closer. Things from which I want the hearers to distance themselves can involve appropriate movement as well. Again, our visual perception is quite acute: dramatic movement can happen within a radius of a few feet.

Whether you preach in the pulpit or nave, learning to stand still is important for physiological and spiritual reasons. The physiological reasons for standing still are the easiest to understand. If you are not nervous when you preach, you may not be taking it seriously enough. "Nerves" are the energy from a frustrated "fight-flight" mechanism, that response which we have inherited from a day when organisms had a simple set of responses available to them. The forest burns, Bambi smells smoke and becomes startled and fearful; adrenalin flows; Bambi runs. We cannot run, we must stay there and preach the sermon: the impulse is frustrated, but the adrenalin remains and we have to do something, so we pace, rock, twist our hands, shift our eyes, and fidget. Rather than to display these behaviors it is possible to let the nervousness, or the energy that underlies it, work for you. By standing with your heels about a foot apart (more if you are tall, less if short) and the toes turned outward at about 20 degrees, you effectively lock your hips and provide a stable base for your torso. Something else happens: all that energy that was streaming out past your hips through your feet is now frustrated there as well. "Trapped" above your hips, the energy now animates arms, head, and face. Standing still makes you a livelier preacher.

I originally learned this technique in one of those Madison Avenue training centers where the goal was simply "effective communication," but in a dozen years or so have come to find in it a spiritual value as well as technical help. As the deacon finishes reading the gospel and I get ready to preach, as I plant my feet for the sermon, I remember and let myself feel the rootedness that preachers have in the gospel. From those roots I let myself feel rising through my legs strength, joy and confidence in proclamation. Being essentially an introvert (one of Garrison Keillor's "shy persons"), I also let myself feel the energy of the Christian community, remembering that everyone in the room wants the sermon to be engaging and useful, that we are all on the same side. By associating that posture with these feelings, I have conditioned myself to begin preaching with a kind of positive energy, rooted in both divine and human love. Delivery then flows from this essentially quiet but nonetheless very strong experience. It is a way of actualizing and enjoying the prayer that the whole preparation process has been. Once I experience myself as part of this root system, the sermon seems to be flowing through me rather than struggling to get out. It takes less than a second to experience this power and connectedness once the associations have been put in place. While this helps somewhat with my preaching even when I am not well prepared, it is most beneficial as the capstone of a well-integrated sermon process.

For just the same reason it is not helpful to grip the lectern or pulpit. The energy that might produce spontaneous, lively gesturing is frustrated in a way that makes gestures jerky or late: their first component is always letting go (prying loose) the hands from what they were clinging to. Far better to let the hands begin at the sides of the body and come up naturally. The goal is not to have the hands remain at the sides through much of the sermon at all. Rather, we want them to begin there so that they are free to gesture naturally and richly without having to be torn away from the edges of the furniture or disentangled from the white-knuckled death grip of intertwined hands. This is the professional technique that beginning preachers have the most difficulty assimilating. If it is too difficult or uncomfortable to start with your hands at your sides, rather than make an issue of it, lay your hands gently on the pulpit or on top of each other without their grasping the reading desk or each other. They will still be relatively free for spontaneous gesturing.

You Ought to Write That Out!

The test of effective reading of a manuscript is when the response is "you ought to write that out, I'd like a copy." I have encountered only one technique for reading a manuscript which produces that response with regularity. It allows the preacher to read every word of the manuscript and still observe the eye-mouth rule: only talk when you are looking at someone's eyes. Again, we are indebted to business and industry for the technique.

Those who remember IBM "golf-ball" typewriters will remember a type element called "Orator" (competitors produced similar balls called "Presentation," etc.). These large faces were designed to make easier the reading of manuscripts produced in columns. The technique is used by many corporate leaders, and has been employed by several occupants of the White House.

Observe the following guidelines when preparing a sermon for reading:

—No more than five words per line.

—Use large typing element, such as IBM's Orator, or the "expanded" mode in a computer printer.

—Two columns per page.

—Indent five spaces for each new paragraph.

—Skip three lines between sentences; four lines between paragraphs.

—Be sure each page ends with a period.

When first developed, this technique required a lot of typing time. Present day popular word processing programs such as *WordPerfect* and particularly *Microsoft Word* can do almost everything required here automatically. Computer users should *not* justify the right margin. The eye does not need to contend with the extra spaces. If your computer can only print one column at a time, every other page can be folded or cut, and then pasted to form the right column of the previous one. Photocopying the resultant pasteup provides a slightly less bulky manuscript package to manage.

This system is based on the physiology of vision. Our eyes cannot read a typical line of manuscript without moving three times, and we are then still reading only one line at a time. On the other hand, our eyes can take in a surprisingly large amount of information from a vertical column of text which does not require any eye movement. Particularly when the text is a familiar one, the speaker's own work, less than a second's glance can bring into view one to four complete sentences.

After your text has been prepared in columns, read through it several times. On the third time through, use a red pen to make double slashes to mark the ends of the "chunks" of words or phrases you can conveniently take in at one glance. These marks now tell your eyes where to get each chunk of the sermon. Now practice one more time, looking at an imagined congregation, dipping down for text and not delivering it until your eyes are off the paper. Most people who use this technique experience almost complete word-for-word accuracy. Because you have marked exactly where your eye is to go on the paper, you look at the paper far more briefly than those who must translate notes back into sentences, and most people will not even notice the presence of your manuscript. They will ask you if you plan to write it out.

Worth a Thousand Words

Mark Twain was, by modern definitions, dyslexic. He was also determined to succeed on the lecture circuit, giving readings from his works in most of America and much of western Europe. He tells us in his autobiography how he developed a system for reducing each paragraph or section of the story he was "reading" to a series of pictures. Looking at these pictures, with an occasional word or phrase added, enabled him to recall his text almost verbatim and to concentrate on effective delivery, something he could not have done from a manuscript.

Twain's technique, sometimes called "ideographic delivery," is helpful for preachers on at least two levels. In the first place, it is an amazingly effective tool for delivery. Do what Twain did, reducing each paragraph or other unit to a picture or symbol or two. Add words where necessary, and write out any direct quotations. A few practice runs will provide delivery which is nearly as accurate as reading a manuscript prepared in columns.

What is also interesting about this technique is that people who know they will be reducing their manuscript to a page of pictures tend to write more concretely in the first place, making contact with the things of life long before they might otherwise have applied abstract concepts. These picture manuscripts insure that the sermon will be well illustrated in every sense.

This technique may simply not be for you; if so, forget it. On the other hand, if suggesting this practice produces a very strong negative reaction in you, you might wish to ask how well and how often your sermons connect to images and issues that matter to your hearers.

Sermon Notes

An annotated outline is probably the most widely used method of delivery. If you choose to use an outline, practice from it, making more explicit on the page those points which you have trouble recalling with clarity. When practicing from a hand-written outline, it is important to practice with the paper held at the same distance from your eye and read in the same light as will be the case when the sermon is preached.

Preaching Without Notes

Learning to preach from memory is not hard, provided that "from memory" is not understood as rote memorization. To memorize a sermon, practice remembering it the way you wrote it, in structural units.

Recall first what is the main idea, the goal of the sermon. Then remember the introduction that made the point. Recall how you moved to the problem, and what was to happen to the listener in that section. Finally, recall how power was meant to be experienced by those who hear the sermon.

When you can describe the *process* of the sermon in these broad terms, when you know with precision and without hesitation where you are going and what the major points along the way are, it is possible to start remembering the pieces that belong to each part of the sermon.

Set anchors for yourself. I am highly visual and kinesthetic in how I organize my experience. When practicing to remember a sermon I imagine myself in one spot in the church whenever I deliver the introduction, in another for problem, and another (closest to the congregation) for the power. Because the words and the place become fused for me, moving to the spot where the words belong makes recalling them much simpler. If this seems fanciful, the reader is encouraged to watch Johnny Carson's monologue for five consecutive nights. Note the constant pattern of his movements and gestures. He touches his nose to remember one story, clasps his elbow for another, and so on. The writers often finish the material late, and Carson must learn it quickly. Many jokes of his style do not work well on cue cards. He simply "attaches" pieces of the monologue to his body and remembers them. Knowing where you are going and what is to happen on the way is the best path to memorization of a sermon, just as it is the best way to memorize a piece of music.

Here a word to actors is necessary. Those with professional training in the use of the voice and body bring many enviable gifts to preaching. Nonetheless, a number of quite gifted actors have experienced initial difficulty with sermon delivery because they remembered their sermons like scripts and tried to deliver them as a "part." Almost all of them "went up" (lost their lines) in sermon delivery because the relationship to the "audience" is different in the family of a congregation with which the speaker already has considerable intimacy. Actors have recovered quickly when they left behind the notion that they were playing a part in a theater, and, as one actor-preacher put it, thought of themselves as "coming back into church and talking to my friends." Having made this reframe successfully this student delivered something she knew was conceived, written, and delivered in the context of a relationship which is direct and immediate, on which no curtain actually falls. Who she was to be in this case was herself, and in that she found her freedom to preach with or without notes.

Whichever of these four methods of the delivery is employed, practice is essential for good delivery. For the typical preacher, reading a manuscript in columns takes the least practice, and preaching the paperless sermon requires the most. Regardless of the method of delivery, preachers have practiced enough when they are sufficiently familiar with the sermon to be present to and be an emotional and spiritual part of the worshiping congregation.

The Stained Glass Voice

We all have several voices. Children are taught at an early age the difference between their indoor and outdoor voices, and adults regularly employ many. The qualities of volume, pace, pitch, vowel color, and precision of consonants, employed when hailing a cab, making love, addressing the United Nations, or discussing a bad call with an umpire are all quite different, and appropriately so. It is also true that in our culture some voices are considered inappropriate or insincere. Just as preachers avoid shifty eyes and nervous body movements, so it is well to avoid what has been called "the stained glass voice." It seems that about one preacher in twenty has one.

The stained glass voice is one which is a little too concerned or pious for the occasion, a voice which has in it a hint of the unctuous, one which is more emotional or animated than the content of the sermon (or liturgical text) requires. Such a voice typically is too mellifluous: it adds more "e" color to some vowels, and stretches and convolutes certain syllables. In its parody form, this is the voice that makes four syllables out of the word, "Je-e-e-susss." In reality it is the one that is just a little too "special" for what is being said. The stained glass voice has to be avoided because to many listeners it declares the preacher a "phony." To others it is so "comforting" that it insulates them from any transforming encounter with the Word.

The voice used in preaching will be different from the voices used in counselling or making a phone call from an airport. Avoiding the stained glass voice is a matter of making sure that all the elements in the voice are not different from the ordinary conversational tone, making sure that enough of the ordinary you is present in the voice. Often as children we were exposed to an unnatural preaching voice on a regular basis in someone we respected, and are just echoing what memory tells us that preachers sound like. Here ridding ourselves of the stained glass voice is a matter of routinely making and listening to audio tapes until the voice does not sound unreal. Practice until it sounds real, sounds right, to you.

There was a time when it seemed that helping the five percent or so of students who were afflicted with a persistent preaching voice that was not recognizably theirs was a matter of speech therapy. Conversations with struggling preachers in recent years, particularly those who cannot at first even hear the difference or are defensive about it, suggest that the voice is not theirs because the sermon or the role of preacher is not theirs, as though the mind were insisting that there be some protest against an event without integrity. For the first group, insisting that they not preach what they have not internally grasped, and then just having them take what they do believe and "just tell it to us" without imagining it as "a sermon" produces an entirely different delivery, one that hearers found authentic and appropriate. For the second group, even when they come to acknowledge their deep discomfort with the idea of themselves as preachers there is not as clear a pattern, perhaps because the sample is small. A few have found that identifying their inner protest against preaching (or ordination) gave freedom to seek other professions or other ministry. Others have discovered issues of guilt, unworthiness, or passive aggressiveness that required treatment from a mental health professional before the preaching voice changed.

In any event, it is well to tape every sermon and listen to it a day or so after it is preached. Is that how you want to sound? Is your voice appropriate to the material, the audience, and the occasion?

Developing a complex of delivery skills can be very difficult. It is probably better to focus on one at a time, starting with one that you find easy to master, and moving on to the more difficult ones. In time each technique becomes unconscious, part of the nature of the preacher.

11. The Joy of Criticism

 psychiatrist once told one of my colleagues that there are only two kinds of people in the general population: those who admit that they desire the approval of others, and liars. Along with this observation it is helpful to recall the absolute impossibility for everyone to like you and to like each of your sermons. Thus our fundamental desire for approval exists in tension with the equally fundamental impossibility of receiving it across the board. In our less healthy moments, this tension is denied, and we sometimes can become "people pleasers," shifting our principles and behaviors in order to get approval or "strokes" from those around us.

Feedback on our sermons received from within the set of emotional tensions just described is worse than useless: it is dangerous. The preacher who crafts sermons, perhaps unconsciously, in such a way to as get praise, may not be saying what needs to be said. The preachers who craft sermons specifically to avoid "offending" people in the sense of making people not like them, may be denying the essence of their vocation as preachers.

Nonetheless, feedback is essential to growth in preaching. If one is terrified of criticism then that essential ingredient will not be supplied and preaching may atrophy, the energy it should claim being devoted to peripheral tasks of ministry. The only solution to this dilemma is for preachers to reinterpret the phenomenon of criticism, and to take charge of the sharing of feedback.

But She's a Good Person . . .

Most people do not even like the word criticism, even though most will acknowledge that criticism can and often does mean the pointing out of what is good about something. We prefer to have people share their feelings with us rather than give us their considered opinion. It seems to be the perception in our culture that if I offer an opinion about your work, your value as a person is what is actually being evaluated. Such an attitude emphasizes the wrong subjectivity, and misses the joy of being criticized. It is a commonplace that when an idea or pattern of behavior is being discussed, someone will respond: "But X. is a good person." This is to miss the point. Of course X. is a good person: what is being discussed is X.'s work.

The subjectivity exposed in the critical experience is not my subjectivity as preacher or person. The subjectivity central to the critical experience is the revelation of that set of filters and experiences through which the critic perceived what I presented. It is the critic's revelation of what was received across what has been called the "interpersonal gap."

The Gap

Although a shy person, I enjoy the ritual of The Lunch. I enjoy being with one to three people in a quiet setting, sharing food and pleasant conversation. Bonds are formed or strengthened as food and company are shared, and happy events celebrated, all without the serious commitment implied in The Dinner at home. I enjoy inviting friends and potential friends to these agenda-free events.

Other people perceive The Lunch differently: to them there is no such thing as a free one. For them, the expectation is that when the dishes are cleared and the coffee arrives they are going to be hit with something.

Neither of us is especially right, nor is there much to be right about here. Lunch is not among the eternal verities. We have simply had different experiences, and from them formed different attitudes and expectations. The first December after arriving at my present job I invited two other staff members to Lunch because I felt happy about Christmas and them. I had enjoyed working closely with them, and wanted to celebrate a little.

One of my guests apparently had a great time. The other went through the meal avoiding my eyes, making unusually guarded conversation, and finally, when dessert was ordered, asked me, "All right Paul, what's up?" In her world, people invite co-workers to Lunch when they want something from them besides company. In this transaction I could have been insulted or felt rejected. Instead, I have learned from my friend's feedback to announce to people that "there is no agenda" when inviting them to Lunch.

All that "feedback" indicates is what message has been

received. Communicators need to know what message has been received in order to determine whether the one they intended to send has crossed the gap that exists between people, even people who like each other. My intention to celebrate a little with people I found attractive was transmitted through the behavior of inviting them. One of my guests perceived my message through her history of having been fattened up for the kill at lunches with colleagues, and received a message quite other than the one I hoped to send.

If fundamental misunderstandings can happen in something as simple as this event, considerably more misunderstanding is possible when a preacher and a congregation are paying attention to the life and death issues which sermons address. This is why "That was a good sermon," although always welcome, is not a particularly helpful comment. The speaker who offers such praise may have heard something quite other than the preacher intended. Soliciting criticism or feedback is a way of making sure that everything possible is done in the future to communicate the preacher's intent in a way that the majority of hearers can accurately perceive. It is thus also an important way to learn about your audience. Make the critics your teachers and they will give you gifts you cannot buy. That is the joy of receiving criticism.

Taking Charge

The following section proposes a form of discussion which is concerned with data gathering more than it is with judgments about good and bad sermons, one which gives preachers the chance to have respondents teach them. It also addresses the issue of the occasional person who may be a hostile critic.

Choose a panel of respondents who have an hour after

church (and coffee hour) to discuss the sermon with you. It is important to invite people from whom you really do wish to learn, those whose opinion matters to you. This often means people whose spirituality and commitment you respect. In some cases this means people you think you would like to reach more consistently. I have tried to work with panels of six: three people whom I admired in the parish, two whom I suspected I could do a better job of reaching, and one whom I expected to be fairly challenging. The invitation was the same to all: please help me to learn how my preaching is coming across. If it seems necessary, emphasize to them that they are providing you with a chance to learn, and that for the most part you will be asking them "how" and "what" questions, not asking them to "judge" the sermon. This approach lets them know that their response is quite valuable, and also that they will be safe from the possible discomfort of publicly "grading" someone with whom they may have a close relationship. Make it as clear as you can that this will not be a time particularly devoted to discussing the ideas in the sermon—you are available to do that at any time—but a time devoted to helping you improve your technique as one who prepares and delivers sermons.

Most people feel uncomfortable thinking on their feet, so the first ten minutes of the feedback period is devoted to having them organize their impressions. They were asked not to take any notes during the sermon because preachers want to know what hearers recall from the experience. The little form that follows here has evolved through several thousand uses with students and congregations. It is designed to elicit feedback on the issues around which this book is written: preachers seeking other information would of course adjust these questions or replace them entirely. All the questions are on one side of a sheet of paper, again emphasizing that not much writing is needed. When people are seated, thank them for coming, explain again that their recollections are valuable to you in learning to preach more effectively, and distribute the forms and pencils. Announce that we only have about ten minutes to complete this, and that they only need write down enough to help the discussion along. If you think it is appropriate to explain any of the questions, do so before they answer them. While they are filling out the forms, it is well for you to fill one out as well, based on your intentions for the sermon.

Questions for Discussion

1. What seemed to be the main idea of this sermon? The preacher wanted to get you to————:

> *This question tells you what was heard. It is put first because of its fundamental importance, and because most of the time most people do get the Point. The preacher thus explores the rest of the questions knowing that in a basic way the sermon did do its job.*

2. Based on the sermon and its delivery, the preacher feels————about him/herself and his/her life; the preacher feels———— toward you the hearer; God feels————toward you, the listener.

> *In some places it may be necessary to explain that feeling words are emotional words, and that they cannot be followed by "that," and what you are seeking is a comparison between how you presented yourself (even if "I" appears nowhere in the sermon) and how you expect them to be after encountering something about God in your sermon. I have learned more about myself and about preaching from discussing this question than any other in the list. For instance, self-deprecating humor, which I have employed as a kind of we're-all-in-this-together device, has turned out to be counter-productive.*
>
> *The question probes for congruence between what you are and what you say, between how you perceive and represent God.*

3. In what ways did the sermon deal with the day's scriptures?

4. How was the sermon connected to the day's liturgy or the Church year?

> *These two questions allow you to find out the degree to which sermon, scripture and liturgy are experienced as allies. Question Three also allows you to learn the degree to which you are perceived as preaching the scriptures.*

5. What does Christ *do* in this sermon?

6. To get you to do or believe the idea in #1, what encouragement, help, or direction did the preacher offer?

> *These two questions can indicate what the Power of the sermon was (the fifth may also indicate Problem to some extent). They will tell you how much of "your gospel" is coming through to the hearers.*

7. Were the illustrations appropriate or distracting? Were there enough? Too many?

> *An evaluative question, letting you know how well the sermon was connected to experience.*

8. Did the preacher in any way reinforce racism, sexism, or religious bigotry? If so, how?

> *We are looking for something more positive in our preaching, of course, but in its negative form, this question is designed to do two things. It alerts preachers to any unintentional signals they may be sending. The word "reinforce" can also ask respondents to examine their own prejudices. The "religious bigotry" questions encourages us to find ways to differ from other Christians on some issues of form or substance without giving the impression that they hold their convictions with any less sincerity than we hold ours.*

9. Comment on delivery, with attention to
—Posture/movement of the body

—Hands/gestures

—Eye steadiness/contact

—Voice: sufficiency, variety, and pace

—Non-words, grunts, and filler-sounds

—Theological "code" or other perplexing expressions

> *Here we are looking for what worked and also what detracted from effectiveness.*

10. Please add any other comments you think would be helpful. Use the other side if desired. Thank you for your help.

> *There are many other questions and many other issues that one could explore in discussion. These have been chosen because they sample the areas that are of general concern to me in preaching and teaching preaching. The questions are not about whether or not the hearer "agrees" with the sermon, although that data will surface inevitably. The last question is a potential gold mine for starting discussion of content.*

Conducting the Discussion

It is easiest to have someone else conduct the discussion, while you yourself just listen. This is not always possible, so some attention is given to the role of conducting your own session here.

You want in these sessions to get all you can from your respondents, so it is important not to explain or defend yourself. Simply ask people to respond to the questions, speaking only to clarify your understanding of what they report or to summarize and focus. Explaining and defending, natural as these reactions are, shut down your learning because you leave the data-gathering mode. One active role can be useful here, and that is coaching hearers to describe your behavior more accurately. You want the hearer to tell you what you did and how you did it that gave the sermon the effect it had. Thus in the second question, if the respondents generally indicated that you seemed to feel tense about your life, a response from you might be, "What did I do or say that gave you that impression?" After a few responses, ask: "Was there anything else that had that effect on you?" until there are no more answers offered. Thus in response to: "You sound so sarcastic when you preach," ask: "What sounded sarcastic to you?" and: "Was there anything else that sounded sarcastic?" until all data are gathered. You thus train hearers to be specific and give yourself enough data to make a decision and take action: if you agree with their criticism, you will have some idea how to correct the problem. At this point, do not discuss the content of their response, but when you are sure the well has been pumped dry, thank them and move to the next questions.

For the most part the data gathered by this technique will be quite appropriate and immediately useful. Sometimes the coaching of behavior description reveals issues which must be addressed privately. A parishioner once offered, "Father, your sermons are so boring." My sermons have been called many unappreciative things, but not usually boring, so my defenses were up over my head. As my mind raced for a comeback, I saw written in red at the top of my copy of the response sheet, in underlined capitals, the words I usually put there, "data only." I was able, although somewhat tremulously, to ask "What makes them boring?" The answer was equally generalized, and began "You never preach about. . . ." As she went on, her criticism became more and more a statement of her own pain. To have discussed it in the group would have sidetracked the purpose of the meeting, subjected her to unfair public scrutiny, and perhaps have scared off other participants. Thus the response to her was "Thank you. Any other comments under number ten?"

After the session was over it was possible to make an appointment with her to discuss her issue.

It is important that positive comments and simple praise also be reduced to behavior description. It is hard to do at first, but learning to respond to vague praise in appropriate circumstances, "What did you like about it" is a way to find out what you are doing right.

When you have gone through the whole list, when everyone has had a say, it is well to summarize and possible to respond. A summary might be: "Let me see if I have heard you correctly. All of you heard my goal as getting us to imitate Jesus' courage in the face of injustice. Most of you thought I felt comfortable with myself and that I felt toward you as friends and fellow pilgrims, and that God wants to support and guide us in our progress. You seemed to think I explained today's gospel fairly well, but thought I could have made a clearer connection between my point and where we are in Lent. You heard me say that Jesus shows us how to act and is with us as we try to follow him, that his resurrection and presence with us give us our real courage. Some of you wished I had been a little more specific about how we can make ourselves more aware of that presence. You thought that there were enough illustrations, but that first one was a little too short: you wanted to know more about how it came out. You thought there were no reinforcements of prejudice, and some of you liked the fact that an immigrant was used as a good example. You generally thought the delivery was all right, but some of you thought I looked away when saying things that made me uncomfortable. Under number 10 you mostly said you liked the sermon, but some of you thought the topic needed to be treated more specifically in terms of our town. Is that a fair summary?"

If it seems necessary to explain something, it is not productive to comment on the hearers' ability to perceive. Stick to what you can say with authority, namely, what your intentions were. Thus "I noted that three of you thought that the story about the bishop was sarcastic, and I appreciate your pointing that out. My intention in that story was to show how we all have our own point of view in any situation, and I will certainly look at it again. Thank you all for your help. It means a great deal to me. Have a good week."

Fogging the Hostile Critic

Every now and then someone really is out to get you, and they may not even know it on a conscious level. They may have had a bad day, may have been confronted with a truth they do not wish to face, may be angry with you about something unconnected to the sermon, or simply may not like you. In addition, some people detect in those they perceive to be "people pleasers" a potential victim and strike as instinctively and unreflectively as a cat pounces on its prey. As a rule, these critics seem to be unhappy about something that is really far removed from the preacher of the sermon, hard as this is for the preacher to believe at the time the criticisms are launched. Finally, some people are hostile for reasons which have nothing to do with you or with the sermon.

There is no point in fighting with these people. Such a response sidetracks the group and inappropriately shifts the center of attention from your sermon to this critic's agenda. There will almost certainly be in the room people who are made very uneasy by conflict of any kind. They will be lost to the work of the group if the stream of negativity is not headed off. Others will simply follow the hostile critic's lead, and a negative cycle will be in place.

This does not occur often, but on the rare occasion when

it does, the cycle must be stopped in a way that does not damage the group or the preacher. The best response to this sort of criticism is what Manuel Smith calls "fogging."[42] Fogging is named for Smith's observation that a dense cloud or fog bank does not punch back, nor is it moved by an attack. It just sits there uninjured. Fogging's main technique is agreeing with the truth in the speaker's critical statements. You agree with only that which is true for you. The person fogging acts as though the critic means well and speaks some truth. Virtually anything and anybody can be improved, and *it costs you nothing* to admit this. Thus, to "Your sermons are terrible," one can respond quite honestly, with what is *true for you*, "You're right, my sermons could be better." The hostile critic is armed to the teeth, and is expecting a fight. A response such as this, said without sarcasm or irony, has a visibly disarming effect, and returns control and focus of the group to its rightful place. Sometimes there is nothing in the criticism which is true for you, but you need to fog or the session will become destructive. Then the fog is, "From your point of view, that does make sense," or more simply, "You may well be right."

Fogging is a technique of last resort, and is rarely necessary. Knowing how to do it means you will never be working without a safety net, however.

Using What You Learn

Most people take the responsibility of giving feedback quite seriously, and most of the responses you get will be of high quality. Nevertheless, it would not make much sense to change

---

[42] See Manuel Smith, *When I Say No I Feel Guilty*. (New York: Bantam, 1985).

one's preaching style based on one encounter with a response group. Scopes on a rifle are not changed based on a single shot, perhaps a stray. A target shooter only adjusts sights when all shots are gathered in a consistent group. If several sessions with a response group indicate that you have trouble making the Point clear within a mass of interesting but distracting illustrations, then it may make sense to go to work on economy and focus. If several sessions indicate delivery problems, work on them. If two or three items consistently surface as problems, most people will probably do better to work on them one at a time, starting with the one they believe to be most important. Possibly one item in delivery and one item in sermon construction can be addressed in the same several weeks.

With respect to the sermon as a whole, sometimes critics are wrong, sometimes they are right. What they are always right about is what they heard and how they reacted to it. Critics of our sermons give us major clues as to who our listeners are and how they hear what we have to tell them. They are gifts to us as we sit down to start the prayer which becomes the next week's sermon.

12. Postscript

ermons are meeting places of theology and life. My thesis has been that effective preaching in the liturgical assembly, when it helpfully connects the day's liturgy and its theology to our private and corporate lives, is one of the answers to the current religious crisis. Christians thus see the reason for the church's programs and position as the same reason that they come to church: the gospel is the power of God and the key to realizing human destiny. Thus preachers are urged to preach only what they themselves believe, to preach only on issues that matter to people, and to preach in a way that allows hearers to appropriate and use that power of God. To do this convincingly, preachers need to know that power. Accordingly, I have stressed the need for preachers to develop an integrated homiletical spirituality. Within a pattern of prayer and contemplation authentic preaching grows and blossoms. What makes it possible for everyone to be a good preacher is that good preaching stems from the preacher's open-

ness to God in scripture, prayer, church, and sacraments. Developing the ability to reflect on one's life and relationships in that context is what makes the preacher. Once this spiritual discipline is undertaken thoroughly, the rest is a matter of organization and writing technique. I have heavily emphasized technique because I believe that skill is the basis on which aesthetic acts are built: when the technique is mastered and becomes unconscious, what happens next is usually art.

Mark Twain ended a lecture by saying "These are my principles. If you do not like them [pause] I have others." I do not share that luxury, and these pages have been as much testament as textbook. If what this book contains has prompted ideas important to you which you would like to share, or if you have experienced preaching in another way about which you think I should know, I should very much like to hear from you. I can be reached at 409 Prospect Street, New Haven, CT 06510.